Doing a Literature Search

A Comprehensive Guide
for the Social Sciences

Chris Hart

SAGE Publications
London • Thousand Oaks • New Delhi

First published 2001.

Reprinted 2002, 2003 (twice)

 SAGE Publications Ltd
6 Bonhill Street
London EC2A 4PU

SAGE Publications Inc.
2455 Teller Road
Thousand Oaks, California 91320

SAGE Publications India Pvt Ltd
32, M-Block Market
Greater Kailash – I
New Delhi 110 048

British Library Cataloguing in Publication data

A catalogue record for this book is available
from the British Library

ISBN 0 7619 6809 1
ISBN 0 7619 6810 5 (pbk)

Library of Congress catalog card number 2001–131325

Typeset by Mayhew Typesetting, Rhayader, Powys
Printed in Great Britain by The Alden Press, Oxford

Contents

List of figures and tables

FIGURES

TABLES

Preface

This comprehensive reference guide will give you the tools and methods to search the literature effectively, using manual and computerized methods, in order to identify useful books, articles and statistics and many other sources of information – it will help you to find information necessary to your research.

This is a detailed guide to searching the literature on any topic within the social sciences, humanities and arts for both academic and work-based research. It will

- provide you with a **quick reference source** to resources (print and electronic abstracts, indexes, guides and gateways) and a **comprehensive guide** to planning and conducting a literature search that will include robust and reliable referrals to other sources, organizations and texts;
- show you **how to manage** the data and information that your search will generate;
- provide you with a clear and concise introduction on how to undertake a **quick review** and a **comprehensive review** of the literature;
- show you how the **tools for locating items** are organized and how you can use them to find literature relevant to your topic;
- show how to **identify key items** in the literature;
- provide lists of **key reference materials** both printed and electronic, especially URLs (Uniform Resource Locators) and titles of guides to the literature;
- show you how to use **computerized methods** to search and organize your findings;
- show you **how to cite references** and how to construct professional bibliographies.

This book can be used as

- a guide enabling you to do a **quick (indicative) search** of the literature

or

- as a guide enabling you to do a **comprehensive search** of the literature.

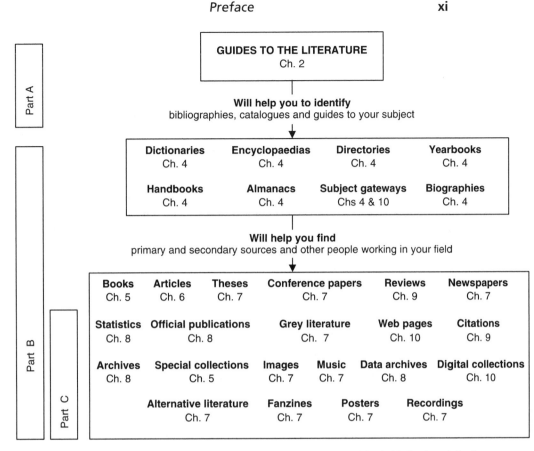

GUIDES TO THE LITERATURE
Ch. 2

Will help you to identify
bibliographies, catalogues and guides to your subject

Dictionaries	Encyclopaedias	Directories	Yearbooks
Ch. 4	Ch. 4	Ch. 4	Ch. 4
Handbooks	Almanacs	Subject gateways	Biographies
Ch. 4	Ch. 4	Chs 4 & 10	Ch. 4

Will help you find
primary and secondary sources and other people working in your field

| Books | Articles | Theses | Conference papers | Reviews | Newspapers |
| Ch. 5 | Ch. 6 | Ch. 7 | Ch. 7 | Ch. 9 | Ch. 7 |

Statistics — Official publications — Grey literature — Web pages — Citations
Ch. 8 — Ch. 8 — Ch. 7 — Ch. 10 — Ch. 9

Archives — Special collections — Images — Music — Data archives — Digital collections
Ch. 8 — Ch. 5 — Ch. 7 — Ch. 7 — Ch. 8 — Ch. 10

Alternative literature — Fanzines — Posters — Recordings
Ch. 7 — Ch. 7 — Ch. 7 — Ch. 7

Part A
Part B
Part C

Familiarizing yourself with the sequencing of this figure will help you search both this book and the literature

Figure A   *The bibliographical framework used in this book*

This book assumes no previous knowledge of literature searching, but it is structured in such a way that the basic advice can be skipped by the more experienced researcher. The book encapsulates all levels of searching, with detailed information and advice and occasional tips for both under-graduate and postgraduate students.

The basic premise of this book is the concept of *bibliographical framework* (structure). This is a framework by which materials are organized. Each type of material, for example books or journals, is organized according to a bibliographical framework. Once you understand this concept you will be able to locate materials in any subject field, even fields in which you have little or no prior knowledge. This is possible because each subject field has *access tools* that are similar. These are tools which organize in a systematic way the content of a subject: so if you are familiar with the generic principles of the bibliographical tools then you can search nearly all subject fields across the social sciences, arts and humanities. Figure A shows the basic structure of the bibliographical framework used in this book.

For effective literature searching some competences must be acquired. You will need basic knowledge of the working of the academic library, to prepare a plan to search out what you are looking for and to know how to manage what can be an intricate and complex task. Remember that a competent literature search demands reliable, clear and consistent management of information. Working through Part A (Chapters 1 to 3) and familiarizing yourself with the Appendices will help you here. You will need to search the main types of the literature efficiently and effectively. Part B (Chapters 5 to 9) provides a sequential organization to a search. Each chapter deals with a specific type of literature: for example Chapter 5 deals with books and Chapter 6 with journal articles. Each chapter gives information on the *main* reference sources that need to be searched to find the literature available. The reference sources are arranged by broad subject areas within the social sciences, arts and humanities. In Chapter 4, for example, the core indexes and abstracts for searching sociology, psychology and other subjects are listed. Chapter 2 is pivotal to the information contained in Chapters 4 to 9. It provides information on how to identify specialized reference sources on each type of material. You will find that information technology – abstracts and indexes on CD ROMs are available via online hosts and the Internet and are mentioned in every chapter. Part C (Chapters 10 and 11) moves on to focus on information communications technology, explaining how it works and how it can be used for advanced searching.

Apart from guidance material, the book is packed with reference materials (source lists and URLs) which any student will find useful. Chapters 4 to 10 contain material that will almost continually be referred to throughout the search process. The book is therefore a reference guide and a handbook to keep beside you when doing your search.

Each chapter includes a range of sources and resources which you can use to find materials. These lists are not exhaustive but indicate the main sources that most researchers use and that lead to other sources. The style used for the citations is different from those recommended in Appendix 4. Here the title is given first because most libraries arrange reference materials, such as indexes and abstracts, alphabetically by title. So the citation style used here should help you to look for sources and resources in your library and when searching the Internet, online databases and CD ROMs.

An important point to remember is that searching is an iterative process between guides and data and primary sources. I hope you will find this a book to come back to again and again to support and inform your search, and that it will contribute to the successful outcome of your research project. Enjoy your literature search!

SYMBOLS USED IN THIS BOOK

The following symbols appear against most of the sources and resources cited:

▣ = journal-type publication
⊙ = CD ROM publication
⌂ = Internet and/or web page source/publication
☎ = online source
📖 = book

Acknowledgements

This, the second in a series of books aimed at the research student and contract researcher, owes much to the same people who gave feedback on *Doing a Literature Review: Releasing the Social Science Research Imagination* (1998) and who are currently looking at *Doing your Research Project* (forthcoming). In particular, I would like to thank David Kane, Sandra Foulds and Mo Bains, who continue to give honest and useful feedback when undertaking their own literature searches and reviews for their doctoral research. Thanks go to Lynne Slocombe for advice on structure and Susan Worsey for arranging the copyediting and production. Thanks also go to Karen Phillips and the editorial team at Sage for their help and assistance. Finally, thanks go to Beverley who put up with the mess and use of space that this kind of book generates.

Chris Hart
Kingswinford 2000

Part A

BASIC KNOWLEDGE: ORGANIZATION OF THE LITERATURE, PLANNING TECHNIQUES AND SEARCH MANAGEMENT

1

The purpose of searching the literature

This chapter will show you:

- the different items that make up the literature
- how to do a quick (indicative topic analysis) search of the literature
- how the literature is organized in, and accessible through, libraries
- where the search links with the review of the literature

WHY SEARCH THE LITERATURE?

A search of the literature is an essential part of every research project. There are two areas to be searched when you are beginning a research project:

- the literature relevant to the topic;
- the literature on research methodology and data collection techniques.

As a researcher you need to become completely familiar with your topic. This means searching out, obtaining and then reading as much as possible in the time you have available. The literature on your topic will be made up of different kinds of material, including books, articles and theses. Figure 1.1 shows the two main kinds of literature to be searched and indicates what benefits each brings to the planning of a research project.

Analysing the literature can have as much intellectual and practical value as collecting first-hand data. A thorough critical evaluation of existing research often leads to new insights by synthesizing previously unconnected ideas, and can provide methods for the collection of data and suggest solutions tried in similar situations. An analytical reading of the literature is an essential prerequisite for all research. It is especially important to have read the literature if you are aiming to collect raw data. Table 1.1 itemizes the kinds of material that form the literature.

You need to know about and understand how other researchers have approached your topic, how they framed their research problem and how

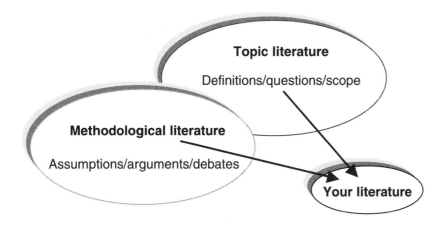

Figure 1.1 *Two kinds of literature*

they went about the business of designing tools to collect appropriate data. Figure 1.2 shows how the two types of literature identified in Figure 1.1 can be used to develop a topic for your own research and help you to write a research proposal.

Reasons for searching the literature
There are at least five good reasons why you should search the literature when beginning your research project. A search of the literature:

1 will help you to identify work already done or in progress that is relevant to your work;
2 will prevent you from duplicating what has already been done;
3 will help you to avoid some of the pitfalls and errors of previous research;
4 will help you to design the methodology for your project by identifying the key issues and data collection techniques best suited to your topic;
5 will enable you to find gaps in existing research, thereby giving you a unique topic.

With a good working knowledge of how the literature is organized, and can be accessed, a comprehensive search can be done in a lot less than six months and a good indicative (i.e. quick) search can be done within a week. Shortly we will see how to do the quick search.

Table 1.1 *Main types of literature*

Books Tend to be published some time after the research on which they are based.	• Treatise and monographs	Thorough treatment of a specific topic; often key texts for that topic.
	• Anthologies (readers)	Collected papers or articles on a topic in one, usually edited, book.
	• Textbooks	General overview of a topic or discipline highlighting main ideas, developments and authors.
	• Reference books	Factual in content; meant for consultation to find sources and definitions.
Articles Time scale from research to publishing is often much less in journal literature than books. Journals contain recent materials on a topic.	• Refereed journals	Articles have been scrutinized (refereed) by peers and evaluated as of a standard suitable for publication.
	• Non-refereed journals	Articles have not been subject to peer assessment and may not be of the same standard (i.e. reliable and valid) as refereed articles.
	• Popular periodicals and newspapers	Popular periodicals and newspapers are generally unreliable sources of information but can provide overviews of debates and issues.
Reports When produced by a private organization they are rarely available to the public. Reports by public organizations more readily available direct from the organization.	• Research reports	Usually published by organizations detailing research from a specific project.

Conference literature

- Published proceedings

Papers and talks given at conferences, symposia and other meetings often provide the latest findings and argument on an issue or problem. Professional organizations and associations often publish conference papers in proceedings. Papers in proceedings which have been subject to referee are more reliable than those which have not.

Many hundreds of conferences are arranged each year.
Many papers given at a conference are never published but are sometimes available from the author.

- Non-published papers

Conferences arranged by non-professional bodies often do not publish the papers given at their conference.

Official and legal publications

- Statistics

Annual, occasional and decennial statistical data available on most areas of government activity.

- Patents and trademarks

Mostly based on technical and scientific developments, they provide sound historical records of developments.

- Standards

Standards on manufacturing processes and services are mostly based on scientific and technical issues.

Substantial amounts of information are published by governments and other official bodies such as the EU and the UN.
Very diverse in nature and availability.
The UK government publisher HMSO publishes only 30% (approx.) of government publications.

Reviews

- Book reviews

These provide information on the ways others, often peers, have assessed and evaluated the contribution and quality of a publication or piece of research.

Most books and academic works are reviewed in the journal literature.

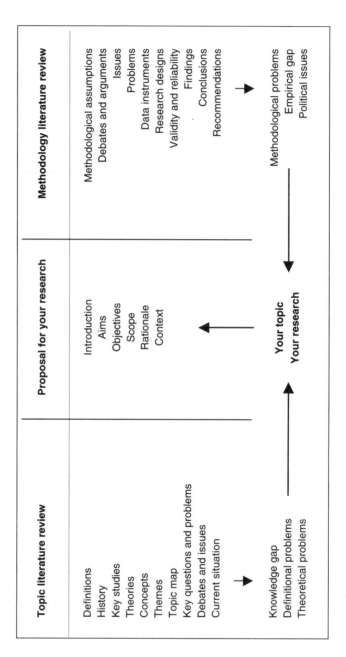

Figure 1.2   *The literature and your research topic*

Table 1.2 *Literature for different project levels, related to search time*

Level	Literature	Search time
Undergraduate	Books, articles, statistics	8–12 weeks
Master's	Books, articles, statistics official publications	12–18 weeks
Doctoral	Books, articles, statistics official publications, reports, conference papers, theses	18–30 weeks

SEARCH TIMES

The process of literature searching and analytical reading can be time consuming. For a Master's thesis, for example, the search of the literature and reviewing might require three to six months to complete satisfactorily. Table 1.2 gives an idea of the minimum scope and time required for literature searching and reviewing for projects at three broad levels.

The time required will, of course, depend on many factors including the purpose and objectives of your project and the nature of your topic. For the two main types of research project, the 'academic' and the 'work based', a search and analysis of the literature in many cases forms the starting point for the research itself. The academic project normally has the purpose of investigating the usefulness of a theory or concept. It aims to critically discuss and evaluate an issue or methodological problem, resulting in some conclusions about the current state of a position or approach. The work-based project will normally be practically oriented, aiming to find the causes of a real life situation deemed to be a problem or in need of improvement. It may involve looking to see how changes to an organizational procedure, structure or service could bring about a desired change. In both cases a search for relevant literature will help you: for an academic project it will show you examples of good practice in argumentation and analysis and for a work-based project it will provide examples of good practice in the evaluation of policy and practices.

> **Tip:** *remember that not all research you find will be good, i.e. reliable, valid and scholarly.*

SEARCHING AND REVIEWING

Searching is not separate from the review of the literature or your research. The review of the literature often continues throughout a research project. Whether your project is academic or work-based, a review of the literature will help give coherence to your project. You should be able to use your analysis to discuss various aspects of research relevant to your topic throughout your project. The use of the topic and methodological literature in different parts of a project is shown in Figure 1.3.

Searching, reading and thinking are embedded in all stages of a research project. A good literature search demonstrates the ability to search, identify and select materials relevant to the topic and which need to be reviewed at a level appropriate to the project. This means all relevant indexes, bibliographies and databases must have been searched in an intelligent way. The keys to a successful search are: planning the search, acquiring knowledge of the tools by which knowledge is organized and made retrievable, maintaining accurate records, selecting potentially useful items and reading them to extract relevant information, including argument, data, theories, concepts and definitions.

> **Tip**: *for guidance on reviewing the literature see the companion to this book Doing a Literature Review (1998).*

Without an appropriate search of the literature your project may lack the breadth and depth of understanding expected for your level and type of project. This book will introduce you to much detail on how to search, but to give you a feel for the process as a whole (especially if you are new to searching) read through the following worked example on a quick search.

WORKED EXAMPLE: THE QUICK SEARCH

There are many occasions when a quick search of the literature is needed. For example, when writing a proposal for your research project you may need to get the gist (overview) of the topic and indicate what are the main sources on the topic. The following example is from psychology but its principles are equally applicable to other disciplines and will help you to plot an effective course through the maze of sources that organize the literature.

If we assume that a quick search might take about 4–5 days then you will not normally have time to obtain conference papers and theses, or order materials from other libraries. Follow the six stages and you should find sufficient materials on your topic for you to write an indicative review of the literature.

Stages in the quick search: *Psychology*

Stage 1:   Familiarize yourself with the library
Stage 2:   Define your topic
Stage 3:   Use the quick reference section of the library
Stage 4:   Search for books in the library
Stage 5:   Search for articles in journals held by the library
Stage 6:   Search the Internet

The literature	Elements of your project	Relationship to the topic and methodological literature
	Rationale	Reasons for investigating the topic – e.g. gap in existing knowledge and understanding; need to enhance definitions; need for theoretical development; lack of empirical studies – developed out of the literature. Discuss how your problem definition relates to the literature in order to justify your topic.
	Research design	Methodological assumptions, purpose, aims, objectives, scope, data collection instruments, method(s) for analysis – developed out of the literature. Discuss how your research design relates to previous research and methodological assumptions for the study of the topic to rationalize your design.
	Findings	Your findings – discuss how they relate to other findings in the literature in terms of what they add to our understanding and how they attend to the issues of validity and reliability of the research design.
	Discussion	Discuss how your research relates to or integrates with existing theories, definitions, and concept use, including your own research design with that used by others.
	Conclusions	Evaluate your research in terms of a brief discussion of the advantages and disadvantages of employing certain methodological assumptions, definitions, concepts, highlighting the degree of validity and reliability of your research design and how your findings contribute to an understanding of the problem.
	Recommendations	Based only on the conclusions, if appropriate, make recommendations for resolving a problem, improving a situation or indicate what further research might be necessary in the area.

Topic literature

Methodological literature

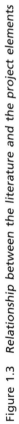

Figure 1.3   *Relationship between the literature and the project elements*

Stage 1: Familiarize yourself with the library

Find out where the books and journals on psychology are shelved or stored. Books on psychology might be shelved under the following headings:

- Psychology
- Sociology
- Educational psychology
- Psychology and medicine
- Mental disorders

> **Tip:** *walk around and make a plan of the library.*

Journals on psychology are normally shelved along with journals of all disciplines in alphabetical order. The library will have a list of the psychology journals it has. Remember that some of these will be print versions and others might be in electronic form, available through the Internet or CD ROM. Use the library's journal list to identify any that might be relevant to you. Some journals deal with very broad topics such as:

> **Tip:** *ask the librarian for a list of journals stocked by the library.*

- *American Psychologist*
- *British Journal of Psychology*
- *Psychological Record*

Other journals concentrate on particular areas of psychology such as:

- *Child Language Teaching and Therapy*
- *Journal of Abnormal Psychology*
- *Journal of Genetic Psychology*

Stage 2: Define your topic

In order to provide a focus for your search write a profile (see Appendix 3: 'Literature search profile') to guide what you will look for. Do this by:

1 writing down your topic, e.g. 'history of mental institutions';
2 specifying the time period, e.g. 1700–1950;
3 specifying the country, e.g. United Kingdom. Therefore, only materials about institutions for the mentally ill and disabled in the UK are to be sought;

> **Tip:** *use a thesaurus to build up your vocabulary of the topic.*

4 listing the key words, e.g. mental, hospitals, insanity, institutions. Use books from the quick reference section of the library to provide a list of key words and terms that you can use. Remember that some terms may no longer be in common use, e.g. insanity, and that some words and phrases may be technical.

Stage 3: Use the quick reference section of the library

Each academic library and most large central public libraries have a quick reference section. This usually contains dictionaries, encyclopaedias, guides and bibliographies along with other reference materials. You will also find discipline-specific reference books there. Do the following when starting out on your research.

First, consult encyclopaedias and dictionaries such as:

- **Blackwell encyclopaedia of social psychology**.
  Manstead, A.S.R. (ed.) Oxford: Blackwell, 1995. 📖
- **Companion encyclopaedia of psychology**.
  Coleman, A.M. (ed.) 1994. 📖
- **Psychological dictionary**.
  3 vols. Duijker, H.C.J. and van Rijswijk, M.J. London: IUPS, 1978. 📖

By consulting encyclopaedias for your discipline you should get

- background on your topic, e.g. history, origins, arguments, key researchers;
- a list of key words for your search. Remember to use the indexes as these might give a better guide to the different places to look for useful information. The index might also provide further terms for your search;
- references on the topic, e.g. books and articles.

Second, ask the librarian what other reference materials are available for your discipline such as:

- **Psychology: a guide to reference and information sources**. Baxter, P.M. 1993. 📖

This kind of guide will provide a list of dictionaries, encyclopaedias, abstracts and indexes and other reference sources relevant to psychology. Remember that any such guides published before the 1990s will not have references to electronic sources and resources but may list print-based ones which have become electronic in recent years.

Stage 4: Search for books in the library

Using your list of key words and phrases search the library catalogue. Usually this will be an OPAC (Online Public Access Catalogue) that will allow you to search by, 'key word', 'author', 'subject' and 'Dewey Decimal location'.

> **Tip:** *browse the shelves of the library.*

Stage 5: Search for articles in journals held by the library

You can search for articles on your topic using abstracts and indexes for psychology journals and other journals in the social sciences. Indexes give you the information you need to locate a journal article, that is, the title of the article, title of the journal, its author(s), its year of publication, volume and part and page numbers. An abstracting journal will give you the same information and more. It will also give you a short summary of the article (an abstract). Indexes and abstracts are available in printed and electronic form. Some of the main indexes and abstracts for psychology are:

- **PCYCLIT psychological abstracts** ⊙ 🕸

> **Tip:** *see what articles are referenced in general text books on the topic.*

Remember that other indexes and abstracts might also be helpful, such as:

- **CINAHL** (Cumulative Index for Nursing and Allied Health Literature) ⊙ 🕸
- **MEDLINE** (Medical literature) ⊙ 🕸 ☎
- **ASSIA** (Applied Social Science Index and Abstracts) ⊙ 🕸 ☎

Stage 6: Search the Internet

There are now several *gateways* to disciplines available on the Internet. These are services that bring together web sites on a given discipline or topic, and more is said about these in Chapter 10. Popular gateways for searching psychology topics and resources (and other academic disciplines) are:

- **Psycsite**
  (address – http://stange.simplenet.com/psycite/) 🕸
- **Yahoo**
  (address – www.yahoo.com/) 🕸
- **UK web library**
  (address – www.einet.net/galaxy/) 🕸
- **Index of cognitive and psychological sciences on the Internet**
  (address – http://dawnw.essex.ac.uk/~roehl/PsycIndex/) 🕸
- **BUBL Link (150 Psychology: general resources)**
  (address – http://link.bubl.ac.uk/) 🕸

If you follow the six stages you should have sufficient references to books and articles to get you started on a topic.

Table 1.3 *Overview of the literature maze*

Research and information is published and communicated in these types of publication	Different types of publication can be found in these different collections and kind of organization	Published work and data are organized with, and can be searched using, a range of tools
monographs	academic libraries	subject indexes
anthologies	public libraries	subject abstracts
edited works	special libraries	bibliographies
textbooks	national libraries	encyclopaedias
articles	government libraries	dictionaries
theses	museums (public and	year books
official publications	private)	almanacs
legal publications	archives (public and	guides to the literature
trade literature	private)	guides to libraries
conference papers	special collections	guides to archives
editorials	charities	guides to special collections
patents and trademarks	political parties	Internet directories
statistics	commercial organizations	online and CD ROM
ephemera	trusts	databases
	Internet	online database hosts

ACADEMIC COMMUNICATION

You will recall that Table 1.1 (on p. 4) gave a broad-brush approach to the main types of literature. Table 1.3 indicates that there is a huge amount of it 'out there' – a maze – and the example has illustrated one attempt to explore this maze. The remainder of this chapter provides an introduction to some of the principles by which knowledge is organized.

Over the last two hundred or so years the development of libraries has created systems for the collection, storage, organization and retrieval of knowledge and information. Knowing your way around these systems is essential if you are to become fully familiar with your topic.

To make this research knowledge accessible it is necessary to classify and catalogue it – and conventions have evolved for doing this. We will now look at some of them.

How libraries organize knowledge

Using a library, any library, demands knowledge; you need to know how libraries work. The collection, storage, classification and development of professional systems for retrieving information are complex. The knowledge required to manage a library demands a graduate or postgraduate education. The researcher therefore needs to acquire at the very least a working knowledge of the organization of library collections and how retrieval systems access those collections. Even a basic understanding will enable you to articulate your needs in such a way that the librarian can guide you to relevant sources. The first thing to note is that not all libraries use the same systems. Depending on factors such as the type of material in the collection (e.g. books, maps, archive records, images) or country (e.g. United Kingdom, United States of America) different schemes and catalogues are used to arrange and search materials.

The most popular system of classification in the United Kingdom is the Dewey Decimal Classification (DDC) and in the United States of America it is the Library of Congress Classification. Originally designed in the 1870s, the Dewey Decimal Classification scheme continues to be developed and revised. The basic idea is the arrangement of books according to subject content. In the main the scheme does not classify the location at which the books can be found in the library.

> **Tip:** *see Appendix 1 for the 100 classes of the Dewey Decimal Classification scheme and the Library of Congress Classification scheme.*

Thus, there will usually be more than one location for a given topic or subject. For example, the subject 'families' has at present 23 locations in five basic classes: the relative aspects of subjects are distributed among different locations within the scheme. Changes to the scheme have been mainly ones of detail. For example, computer science is a relatively recent discipline and is therefore classified in Generalities. The tremendous growth in the breadth and complexity of knowledge since the 1870s is the main reason for changes to the scheme.

Apart from the basic subject headings the scheme works on the principle of *general-to-specific-arrangement*. The knowledge on subjects is normally divided by form, with each form being subdivided into specific subject content. Figure 1.4 shows the second level of subdivisions for the 300s. By knowing the form of a subject you can navigate your way around the detailed content of that subject, following various leads.

> **Tip:** *see Appendix 2 for the DDC locations of materials on the following subjects:*
>
> Sociology   Economics   Politics
> Government   Literature   Social work
> Media & communications

This ability to follow leads is particularly important for finding literature on research. All researchers need to know about research methodology and about the different techniques for collecting, organizing and presenting data. There is no one section within DDC that is dedicated to methodological knowledge or to the tools of data collection. Texts relevant to these areas can be found in various sections. Figure 1.5 summarizes some sections useful to locating literature on research.

Types of library

There is a wide range of libraries available that most researchers can use. In the United Kingdom researchers have access to one of the best library systems in the world. Through the local public library you can access not only the main national libraries in the United Kingdom but also collections in other libraries around the world.

Useful publications are:

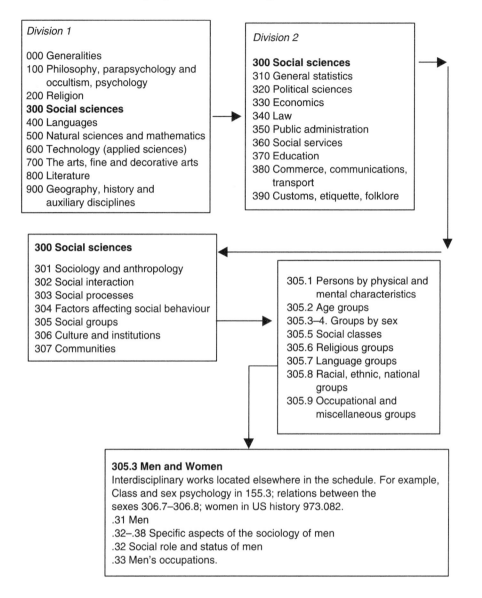

Figure 1.4 *Hierarchical structure in the Dewey Decimal Classification (DDC) scheme*

- **Libraries in the United Kingdom and the Republic of Ireland 2000.**
  26th edn. London: Library Association, 1999. 📖
- **Guide to libraries and information units in government and other organizations.**
  33rd edn. Dale, P. (ed.). London: British Library, 1998. 📖

Technique	DDC class
Questionnaires	001.422
Interviews	001.42
Group interviews	020.72
Observation	001.433
Analysing data	001.4225
Research and development	658.57
Writing research reports	808.06602

Figure 1.5   *DDC's classification of 'research'*

Table 1.4   *Library and information provision in the United Kingdom*

Type of library	Examples
Academic libraries	University libraries
Public libraries	Central public libraries
National libraries	Copyright depositories: British Library, the Bodleian Library, Oxford; University Library Cambridge; the National Library of Wales; the National Library of Scotland; and Trinity College, Dublin
Government libraries	Central Statistics Office Library
Special libraries	Museum of Mankind Library, British Museum, Marx Memorial Library, BBC libraries information research library, sports libraries, picture archives
Commercial libraries	Picture libraries
Public records offices	Public Record Office
Archives	National Motor Museum Archive, Beaulieu
Documentation centres	British Library Document Supply Centre, Boston Spa
Research centres	Data archive at the University of Essex (ESRC)
Association libraries	British Sociological Association, British Advertising Association
Health libraries	Health and Safety Executive Information Centre

- **Guide to libraries and information sources in medicine and health care.**
  2nd edn. Dale, P. (ed.). London: British Library, 1997. 📖
- **Guide to libraries in London.**
  McBurney, V. (ed.). London: British Library, 1995. 📖
- **European Commission libraries site.**
  (address – http://europa.eu.int/comm/dg10/libraries/bibliotheques _en.htm). 📖
- **World guide to libraries.**
  London: Bowker-Saur, 1998. ⊙ 📖 📖

These and other directories list hundreds of libraries in the United Kingdom and give an idea of the scope of some collections as well as providing information on how to make contact with the library.

As a general rule most libraries can be classified into one of three types: academic libraries, public libraries, and special libraries. Every institution of learning in the United Kingdom has a library. University libraries tend to differ in their policies on access and collections. Most are open to members of the institution. External students can normally arrange to use any university library for reference purposes, although a fee may be payable.

> **Tip:** *has your library a special collection that could form the basis for your own research?*

Academic libraries often have special collections, for example Birmingham University has a special collection of local government material and the British Library has a collection of ephemera. Public libraries are open to everyone regardless of their ability to pay. Most large towns and cities have excellent reference libraries. The central libraries of Manchester and Birmingham, for example, have very good collections of social science texts. Special libraries are many and varied; they exist to serve the 'special needs' of particular organizations or associations, such as trade associations (e.g. the Institute of Mechanical Engineers), professional bodies (e.g. the British Sociological Association), research institutions (e.g. the National Institute of Economic and Social Research), museums (e.g. the British Motor Industry Heritage Trust) and the like. Many places, people, languages, cultures, ideas, movements and numerous types of artefact have special library collections dedicated to them. Added to these there are about 1,200 archives and approximately 2,500 museums in the UK containing all kinds of printed material and artefacts. The problem is finding out if there is a special collection on your topic and then gaining access to it. General guides to collections in special libraries and archives include:

- **British archives: a guide to archive resources in the United Kingdom**. 3rd edn. Foster, J. and Sheppard, J. London: Macmillan Press, 1999. 📖
- **Directory of special libraries in Western Europe**. Gallico, A. London: Bowker-Saur, 1993. 📖

Access to these libraries is normally restricted and you will have to make clear to the librarian your reasons for wanting to use the library and abide by whatever conditions exist concerning the use of materials. The advantage of specialist libraries is that the librarian in charge often has very detailed knowledge of the collection.

> *Examples of collections in special libraries in the UK*
>
> | | |
> |---|---|
> | American history | Arab studies |
> | Automobiles | Business history |
> | Celtic language | Communism |
> | Economics | English history |
> | Gypsy literature | Illustrated books |
> | Miners' strike 1984 | National socialism |
> | Oriental studies | Sports |
> | Trade unions | Witchcraft |

At the centre of the UK library system is the **British Library**. Most libraries use the British Library in some way or other. It is Britain's national library and is divided into several divisions, three of which are particularly important to know about. The British Library OPSS (Official Publications and Social Sciences) is a massive collection of contemporary and historical materials and intended for research that cannot be done elsewhere by other means.

Materials can only be read in the reading room and there are strict terms on admission. The British Library National Bibliography Service is responsible for compiling the **British National Bibliography (BNB)**, a catalogue of all published material. Finally there is the British Library Document Supply Centre (BLDSC) at Boston Spa in North Yorkshire. The BLDSC has an unbelievably large collection of books, monographs, reports, conference proceedings, theses, music and translations and can acquire most known items from around the world. Items can be borrowed via an academic library or read in the reading rooms provided at Boston Spa. However, you can only borrow items by making a request through a library.

Tip: *the British Library will do a search for you. Social Science Search is a fee-based service run by the Library's Social Policy Information Service.*

CROSS-DISCIPLINARY SEARCHING AND PERSONAL TRANSFERABLE SKILLS

In this book a broad inclusive approach has been taken to the definition of the social sciences, humanities and arts. The following list gives an idea of the scope of disciplines that make up the social sciences, arts and humanities. This is not exhaustive, it is merely indicative. Archaeology, tourist and leisure studies, sports studies and women's studies are subject areas that might also be included in the list. The thing to note is that apart from those working in Information and library science, students of most subjects are not usually sufficiently trained in the use of tools for literature searching.

Examples of subjects in the social sciences, humanities and arts

Economics	Education	Research
Human geography	Political science	Cultural studies
Social anthropology	Sociology	Community studies
Social policy and administration	Theology	Art
Social statistics	Town planning	Graphics and design
Economic and social history	Literature	Business studies
Linguistics and languages	History of ideas	Human geography
Psychology	Women's studies	Management science
Organizational studies	Education	Communication and media studies

---

Most disciplines have an identifiable knowledge base and this is usually accessible through the tools which organize it. The other is the tools that organize that knowledge base, and knowledge in general. An increase in the number of subjects has led to an increase in the number of tools that

Basic tools of the researcher

e.g. library searching and use of abstracts and indexes, bibliographical construction, record keeping; use of information technology for word processing, databases, online searching and electronic mail, and techniques for the evaluation of research, including refereeing, reviewing and attribution of ideas.

Research design and strategy

e.g. formulation of researchable problems and translation into practicable research designs, identifying related work to rationalize the topic and identify a focus, organize timetables, organize data and materials; understanding and appreciating the implications of different methodological foundations and how to deal with ethical considerations that may arise.

Writing and presentation

e.g. planning, writing, preparing and submitting papers for publication, conferences and journals; the use of references, citation practices and knowledge of copyright; construction and defence of arguments; logic, clear and coherent expression, and understanding the distinction between conclusions and recommendations.

Figure 1.6 *Personal transferable skills*

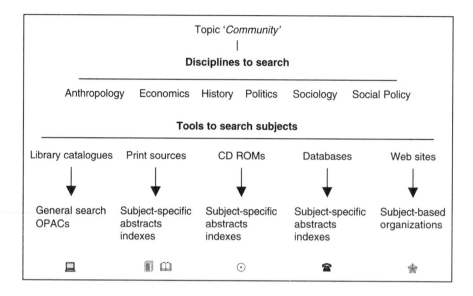

Figure 1.7 *Cross-disciplinary search: 'community'*

organize the knowledge of those subjects. Finding your way around the academic map has become more difficult for students and researchers so it is essential that all students learn how to utilize the resources of the academic environment. Without a knowledge of how to do this you will be unable to effectively complete the personal research work that increasingly makes up the curriculum of higher education. This is because dissertations, work-based projects and Master's theses are used as evidence that you have developed and applied a range of research skills, many of which are common to most disciplines. They are what are called *personal transferable skills* (PTS) and Figure 1.6 indicates the abilities expected from all higher education students.

An element common to these core skills is a thorough understanding of how information is generated, stored and retrieved. This means that to search a literature you need to know about such things as the organization of resources in academic, public and commercial libraries in the world; the use of electronic tools such as JANET (Joint Academic Network), OPACs (Online Public Access Catalogues), CD ROM and the Internet; as well as how to locate sources of information through indexes, abstracts and directories. It is knowledge of these resources and sources that enables you to find information relevant to your needs. Such skills also play an important part in developing cross-disciplinary understanding. This is because if you are competent in searching a literature you can apply the basic principles to any literature regardless of the discipline or topic. Figure 1.7 contains a simplified example of a cross-disciplinary approach to searching for resources on the topic of 'community'.

SUMMARY OF THIS CHAPTER

1 All research benefits from a search of the literature.
2 The search can help prevent repetition and mistakes, and thereby enable you to make positive contributions throughout the project.
3 It is possible to do a quick search based on materials held by your academic library and this can be the foundation of a much broader search with depth.
4 A search across different disciplines will provide insights and broader understanding of the topic and methodologies.
5 A core transferable skill for all researchers is the ability to search the literature efficiently and effectively.
6 A search of the library catalogue or the web does not constitute a literature search.

2

Search preparation and planning

This chapter will show you:

- how to plan for a comprehensive search of the literature on your topic
- how to use guides to the literature
- how to place limits around your search

An effective search of the literature can be done quickly but not in a casual way: it requires planning and attention to detail. To undertake an effective search of sources and thus find sufficient literature relevant to your topic you must use a range of tools, such as *indexes, abstracts* and *catalogues*. To find out which sources might usefully be consulted, you can use the various guides that list the abstracts, indexes, bibliographies and other sources on most topics.

PREPARING YOUR SEARCH

To prepare a search for literature relevant to your topic you need to understand the nature of the tools that enable items to be identified, located and obtained. The disciplines associated with information science have developed a range of tools to organize knowledge. These include library catalogues, indexes and abstracts. There are so many tools that information science and librarianship is a subject discipline as well as a profession in its own right. Given this fact, the researcher may acknowledge that he or she will never be able to gain the knowledge of sources and systems by which information is organized that the professional librarian possesses. Therefore the subject librarian is one of the main sources of information for all researchers. A good librarian can make all the difference to a search for relevant information.

Tip: *remember serendipity – the fortuitous accidental find – that often happens when browsing in the library or carefully scanning bibliographies.*

All searches for literature have some typical features and progress through some common stages. Table 2.1 describes the structure involved in the preparation for undertaking a search of the literature. One thing to note

Table 2.1 *Initial preparation for the literature search*

Task	What to consult and use
1 Define the topic Write down the main topic and what disciplines you think will have had something to say about it.	Consult the dictionaries and encyclopaedias in the quick reference section to develop a list of key words that can be used to search the library catalogue, abstracts and indexes. **Tips:** use the 'Literature search profile' (see Appendix 3) to record key words. Familiarize yourself with the layout of the library, get a list of journals in the library and indexes and abstracts (print and electronic). Record from encyclopaedias key authors and references on your topic. These should be among the first items to be obtained and read.
2 Think about the limits of your topic Limit your search by placing parameters around the time frame (dates), language(s), place and population.	Use materials from the encyclopaedias and dictionaries to define the scope of your topic and to write a working title. Adapt the 'Literature search profile' to write down the criteria for your search – what to include and what to exclude. **Tips:** use limitations to focus your topic and thus give more preciseness to your search. Remember to keep accurate notes on your decisions.
3 Identify the main reference tools for your discipline Identify the main indexes and abstracts and any other reference materials that cover the disciplines for your topic.	Use guides to the literature from the quick reference section of the library to identify relevant indexes and abstracts and reference sources including Internet gateways. Check which reference tools the library holds that you can use. **Tips:** look for guides produced by the library on the different disciplines, e.g. sociology. Make a record of what you intend to search.
4 Think about the housekeeping Design a means of recording what you find and how you will cross-reference materials.	Use ring binders to store notes and index cards to record citations. **Tips:** don't employ information technology at this stage as it is time consuming and because how you need to record information will change and you can't normally carry a PC around with you. Record all activities and cite references in full, as you may have to re-track at a later stage and justify what you have done.
5 Plan the sources to be searched and start your search List the sources you intend to search in the order in which you intend to search them.	Use your notes to construct a list of abstracts, indexes and other reference sources to be searched. **Tips:** start with the obvious and most general sources such as the library OPAC, looking to see if books cited in encyclopaedias are in the library. Keep clear and accurate records of what you have searched and what results were obtained.

is that you have to do some preliminary thinking about what you are doing before you begin the search itself. The other thing to note is that although Table 2.1 represents the process as linear it might better be described as a helical process: you tend to go back and forth between sources following leads, expanding on previously acquired information and validating references. But if you follow the general plan in a systematic way then you can be assured that a thorough search will have been undertaken and that most of the literature relevant to your topic will have been identified. A key task at the start is to sit down in the library to think about how you will manage the search, including keeping records.

There is no set way of going about a search. Where you begin depends on your knowledge of the topic. If you have an advanced understanding of the topic area then only a *state of the art search* may be required. This would mean searching for recent works that probably have been presented only at conferences or in the form of working papers. If, however, the topic is relatively new to you then a quick (indicative) search (see Chapter 1) followed by a full search might be of benefit.

SEQUENCES AND OUTCOMES OF A QUICK SEARCH

Most searches move through a typical sequence, starting with guides to the sources before moving on to a search of the sources themselves. The order of the search will be shaped by the topic, by access to sources and by the level of pre-existing knowledge you have of the topic area. Some topic areas are more established than others. Sociological theory, for example, has a long and complex history that is well documented in an extensive literature. This literature is itself subject to a range of detailed indexes and abstracts.

Tip: *once you have an indicative plan consult your college librarian for advice – they can be very helpful.*

Most, if not all, academic libraries have copies of abstracts and indexes covering the sociological literature. But with a topic like AIDS/HIV the organization of the literature and research on the topic may not be so widely accessible. There are fewer indexes and abstracts, and because they focus on the medical aspects not all academic libraries can be expected to stock indexes and abstracts on AIDS/HIV. They are more likely to be found in institutions with a tradition of medical and biological research. You can expect some recent topics not to have dedicated abstracts and indexes; or they may have only a few institutionally produced indexes. Embryonic topic areas are often classified under more general topic categories: for example many feminist studies are classified under sociology. Therefore a broad and multidisciplinary approach is often needed when searching on your topic.

Figure 2.1 gives an overview of the kind of information that can be obtained from different sources. It shows the logic of a typical search, which is reflected in the bibliographical framework of this book. For most research projects the safest place to begin is with encyclopaedias in the

Task ─────────►	Tools ─────────►	Outcomes
Defining the topic *Chapters 1 & 2*	Dictionaries and encyclopaedias	List of key words. List of key authors, books and articles.
Background knowledge on the topic *Chapter 2*	Encyclopaedias Textbooks in library	Initial outline of the topic, key ideas, people and landmarks. Introduction to the vocabulary of the topic.
Find sources to consult in order to locate relevant literature (e.g. books) *Chapters 1, 2 and 10*	Guides to the literature Subject librarians Internet gateways and directories.	List of abstracts, indexes, bibliographies and reference sources.
Search for books *Chapter 5*	Library OPACs BNB Publishers' catalogues	List of books with bibliographical details.
Search for articles *Chapters 6 and 11*	Indexes and abstracts (electronic and print) Online databases	List of articles with bibliographical details.
Search for theses *Chapter 7*	Dissertation abstracts (electronic and print)	List of dissertations and theses.
Search for conference proceedings *Chapter 7*	Conference proceedings	List of papers in conference proceedings.
Search for statistics and official publications *Chapter 8*	Indexes and abstracts Publishers' catalogues (HMSO)	Lists of statistical sources and organizations. Identification of official publications.
Search for grey literature and research reports *Chapters 7 and 10*	Internet and gateways Research directories	List of items not published. List of research reports and organizations.
Search for reviews of books and research *Chapter 9*	Indexes and abstracts Review journals	List of book reviews and evaluations of research.
Identify core texts *Chapters 1 and 9*	Citation indexes and bibliographical analysis	Map of the links between publications and highlight landmark studies

Figure 2.1 *Working through the literature search tasks and this book*

quick reference section of the library and with a quick search on the library OPAC (catalogue). This will provide a starting point and list of sources to be consulted.

The principal aim of a literature search is to identify material relevant to your topic. Initially the objective is to produce lists of items that are potentially relevant. In Figure 2.1 the main tasks of a search are sketched out, along with the chapters in which they are described in this book. Although this is a simplistic representation of the process it shows how the main objective of producing bibliographies is achieved. But a search does not progress through such clearly defined phases – you do not simply search for books and then search for articles. In each phase you will normally come across references to other types of materials not previously found. For example, if you are searching journal articles and come across a monograph, then this find cannot be ignored.

Selecting relevant items

Tip: *see Chapter 3 for advice on managing your search.*

A search is about locating and managing large amounts of information. Quite often much of what is located is irrelevant or superficial. A search involves a large degree of multi-tasking on several levels using a wide range of tools. On one level you are looking for material on your topic but may, as is often the case, find far too much. So as items are identified, their relevance needs to be assessed. Table 2.2 gives some criteria which should help you to discriminate between relevant and irrelevant 'hits'.

You will constantly be searching and at the same time attempting to evaluate finds (or 'hits' as they are called). This is no easy task: there are no prescriptive methods you can employ to identify key texts (i.e. landmark studies). No manuals exist to tell you what is a core book. There are, however, tools called *citation indexes* (see Chapter 9) and tactics you can employ to identify a core text: this is known as *bibliographical analysis*. Searching involves information management and decision making. The latter is very much a matter of experience in using sets of criteria to identify core and relevant texts which can make your search efficient and effective.

Table 2.2   *Selection criteria*

Criteria	Description of material
Authority	Materials published by a reputable publisher, articles in a refereed journal and theses from reputable universities.
Seminal	Works regarded as having significantly developed the topic.
Currency	Generally past six years for articles and books, excepting seminal works.
Relevance	Topic based, with hits controlled by the search vocabulary, and within the parameters of the aims of the project.

> **Definition:** *core texts*
>
> An item, published or unpublished (e.g. thesis), that has had an important and measurable effect on subsequent work on the topic as a whole or on development of the topic. This item should meet one or more of the following criteria.
>
> - It is empirical work that has not been done before;
> - argues for and shows the use of an existing idea, approach, practice or methodology in a new and different way;
> - brings new evidence or interpretation to bear on an old issue or problem;
> - provides more empirical data on an issue than has previously been available;
> - creates a new synthesis that has not been done before;
> - develops a new area of investigation for a discipline;
> - adds to the understanding of an issue or problem in a way that has not been done before.
>
> (Adapted from: Phillips, E.M. and Pugh, D. (1994) *How to get a PhD: A handbook for students and supervisors.* 2nd edn. Buckingham: Open University Press.

Assuming the initial search has revealed work on your topic, the main outcome of a quick search is a series of lists.

Working your way through the outcomes in Figure 2.1, the following list indicates typical outcomes from an initial search of the literature:

1　A list of books: Books can be categorized as primary research, critical evaluations and interpretations. Books are a source of bibliographies. The bibliographies will show the materials used by the authors to write their books. Some books provide summaries of the topic through reviews of the literature. These give a strong indication of what are taken as the core texts and key ideas in a topic.

2　List of journal articles: Articles will have bibliographies, though these are not usually as long as those in books. Article bibliographies tend to emphasize a particular focus within a topic or a specific dimension of a debate.

3　List of authors: Searching under *author name* might reveal other work by an author. Some authors will have written other texts on the same topic and will be regarded as specialists in the field; they can lead you to works that may not have been published or are difficult to obtain.

4　List of publishers: Some publishers publish on given topics and may have a range of books or even journals that are relevant. Publishers normally provide catalogues of their publications.

5 List of sources: Consultations with your university librarian will have
   resulted in a list of sources available on paper, CD ROM, online and the
   Internet. These will need to be searched more fully at a later stage.
6 List of words: If you have found too many hits then the search may
   have to be narrowed down. Identifying the key words to search under
   can help with this. Conversely, if you have found too few hits then the
   search might benefit from being expanded using a wider search
   vocabulary.

PROGRESSING FROM YOUR INDICATIVE SEARCH OUTCOMES

The results of an initial search can be carried forward into a more detailed
search. The aim of the next phase is to find more journal articles. Some may
already have been noted and recorded from book bibliographies. Articles
cited in books will probably be dated. This is because books take a long
time to write and a long time to get published. This gap in the article
literature therefore needs attention: you must ensure that a search has been
made for recent article publications as well as for other articles not cited in
books. Consulting a range of special abstracts and indexes will show what,
if any, articles have been published on your topic. Like *BNB*, abstracts and
indexes provide sufficient bibliographical information for articles to be
obtained. Once obtained, the articles can be skim-read to assess their
relevance. They can also be used for further references. Most will have a
bibliography in which new items may be found.

It is at this stage that you begin the task of cross-checking bibliographies
from previous searches with each bibliography from each
new article obtained – hence the term, *bibliographical
analysis*. It is common for articles to be found that are not
listed in abstracts and for books to be found that are not in
BNB. You will also begin to come across what is called *grey
literature*. This is work used by an author such as letters, diaries and other
unpublished materials such as theses (we will look in more detail at this
later). Again, if a book is found that was previously unknown to you, do
not ignore it. If it looks relevant – and often you cannot make this decision
on the title alone – it needs to be obtained. The content of the book might
or might not be relevant but it will have a bibliography that should be
examined. This is a process of searching for new items, analysing their
bibliographies and then retrospectively checking for new items to be added
to one or more of your existing bibliographical lists.

> **Tip:** remember to make systematic
> and contemporary notes on your
> search so that others can
> reproduce your search.

The search consists of trawling for as much as possible: it involves
casting a wide net to get yourself started before discriminating between
your 'finds', and mining for detail in what you find. Figure 2.2 shows this
process. In discriminating you begin to follow up leads and mine your
'hits' for the details that will help you construct your literature review and
design your own research project.

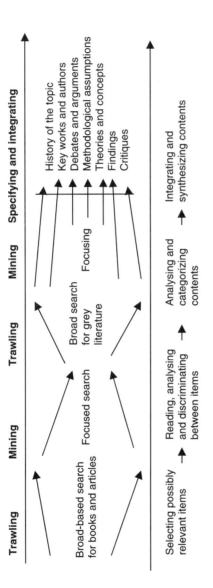

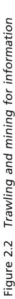

Figure 2.2 *Trawling and mining for information*

Definition: *Grey literature*

Documents written for a restricted audience that are outside of traditional bibliographical controls and are not readily available via conventional channels and which are therefore difficult to identify and obtain.

The search then moves on to look for grey literature. At this stage you are looking for the most current work done on the topic. Recent research on most topics is in the form of unpublished materials such as conference papers, research reports and theses. Some grey literature may already have been found and recorded in the previous two phases. Some of this literature should have been obtained before the start of this phase. Do not wait until you come to a particular phase in the search to obtain materials: order them from the library as you go along, ensuring that you keep up-to-date notes on what has been ordered, what has arrived and what is useful. Most theses and many conferences are recorded in abstracts and indexes such as *Dissertation Abstracts*. In Chapter 7 more is said about finding theses and grey literature. Normally you will find that there are some theses on a topic. If a thesis is recent it may contain research not yet published and have a long bibliography. You can expect that the bibliography of a thesis has been constructed after a thorough search of the literature, so you may find references to books, articles and other theses not found by consulting indexes and abstracts. Thesis bibliographies can help in identifying more obscure books and articles. Like other relevant books and articles these will need to be consulted and their relative bibliographies scrutinized. In this helical search you move up through the literature and then go back, to revisit earlier sources in order to move further into the more detailed areas of the literature. You will constantly be searching abstracts, ordering and then chasing items, and once obtained checking them and looking at bibliographies to see if there are any items not yet found.

GUIDES TO THE LITERATURE

As it is impossible to read everything that appears in the many thousands of journals published each year, abstracting and indexing services exist to provide regular listings of what has been published. In order to maximize the results of the effort put into a search you need to know which abstracting tools need to be searched. First you need to construct a list of relevant reference tools that can be searched. This is because it would be impossible to search all abstracts, all directories, all yearbooks and all other reference sources:

Tip: *remember that many guides now include references to electronic sources.*

for example, in the libraries of the University of Cambridge there are about 460 different abstracts. *Guides to the literature* can be very useful because they provide listings, sometimes with summaries, of the indexes, bibliographies, dictionaries and other sources that have been published on a range of topics. Various guides to the literature are normally found in the quick reference section of the academic library and in many central public libraries. These guides must be consulted before beginning any search for relevant literature. If you do not know where to look for information then as a researcher you will be condemned to wander haplessly around the shelves of the library. Without a list of all the sources that can be consulted you cannot complete a thorough search for related and relevant literature on your topic. Planning what to search is worth the time and effort and is common to all competent research. The guides listed below are recommended starting points. Each provides a massive amount of information on reference sources in the social sciences, humanities and arts. They also provide information on other general guides to the literature.

General guides to the literature:

- **Walford's guide to reference material**.
  Vol. 2. *Social and historical sciences, philosophy and religion*. Day, A. and Walsh, M. (eds) 7th edn. London: LA Publishing, 1997. 📖 ♟

  Vol. 3. *Generalia, language and literature, the arts*. Chalcraft, A., Prytherch, R. and Willis, S. (eds) 7th edn. London: LA Publishing, 1998.

  Walford's is a major tool used by librarians. The volumes list major reference works on national bibliographies; encyclopaedias; essays, theses, reviews; periodicals; institutions and associations; newspapers; government publications; manuscripts; languages; arts and literature. Under the arts, entertainment, theatre and sport there are lists. Most sections give comprehensive references to sources including CD ROM and online databases. 📖 ♟

- **Printed reference materials and related sources of information**.
  Lea, P.W. 3rd edn. London: Library Association, 1990.

  Organized by chapters dealing with most major types of information. Full of useful information on, for example, dictionaries, encyclopaedias, periodicals, theses and reports, local history, bibliographies, community information, official publications and statistical sources. Each chapter has an extensive bibliography. 📖

- **Sources of information in the social sciences**.
  Webb, W.H., Beals, A.R. and White, C.M. 3rd edn. Chicago: American Library Association, 1986.

  Although biased towards American scholarship this is a very useful text covering history; geography; economics and business administration; sociology; anthropology; psychology; education and political science. There is an excellent introduction to the social sciences; references to different schools and methodologies and a guide to the structure of social science knowledge, followed by individual chapters on the different disciplines. Each chapter defines the nature, scope, history and methodologies of the discipline, providing many references. Different elements of each discipline, for example in sociology the sociology of education, mass communications, social problems and so on, are described using the citations. The main reference tools (e.g. abstracts) and specialized sources for each discipline are also described with references for further reading. Lists other general and specific guides to social science literature. 📖

- **Classical studies: A guide to the reference literature**.
  Jenkins, F.W. Englewood Cliffs, NJ: Libraries Unlimited, 1996.
  Gives a broad coverage, including philosophy, civilization and philology, with details of many useful sources for the humanities along with bibliographies. 📖

How to use the guides to the literature

Not all libraries stock all the guides to the literature. The first task is to find out what guides are available from your local reference libraries and academic libraries. Make a list of these. If a particular guide you require is not available locally then order it through the inter-library loan service. As a student of a university you can ask your university library to order items from the British Library or from most other academic libraries in the UK. Remember that inter-library loans take time to be processed and are expensive. As the number of guides can be bewildering, consider finding and consulting subject-specific guides such as the following on your topic.

Subject-specific guides to the literature:

- **Political science: a guide to reference and information sources**.
  York, H.E. Englewood Cliffs, NJ: Libraries Unlimited, 1990. 📖
- **How to find out in psychology**.
  Borchardt, D.H. and Francis, R.D. Oxford: Pergamon Press, 1986. 📖
- **How to find information – environment**.
  Owen, P.S. London: British Library, 1998. 📖
- **How to find source materials: British Library collections on the history and culture of science, technology and medicine**. Summers, A. London: British Library, 1996. 📖
- **Effective use of health care information**.
  Merry, P. (ed.). London: British Library, 1997. 📖

Once you have access to a range of subject guides, systematically interrogate each for reference sources that are not listed in this book. In the chapters that follow the emphasis is on the basic reference tools and not those dedicated to particular sub-topics. For example, if the topic you are searching is

Tip: *the British Library and Library Association often publish guides to different subjects.*

'romance literature' then some of the general tools in *literature* (e.g. Modern Language Association abstracts of articles in scholarly journals) will be of help. To find out what other specialist references sources exist, consult the general guides to the literature.

WORKED EXAMPLE: USING WALFORD

If we take 'French romance literature' as an example the general guides will provide a number of pieces of useful information. First they will give you an idea of the scope of the topic. Looking at entries under 'romance literature' shows that the topic has a large literature. Sources are multi-disciplinary, in many languages and cover a very wide range of authors. Even a rudimentary glance at the following example gives you an idea of the typology of the topic. You can use this to think about how to define the particular aspect of the topic that interests you. The guides will also provide a working list of the types of sources you should be attempting to consult.

Consulting *Walford: guide to reference material* Vol. 3 (1998), you will find a guide to reference materials on literature. Figure 2.3 shows the general structure of the section on 'literature'.

Walford: organization of reference sources for literature

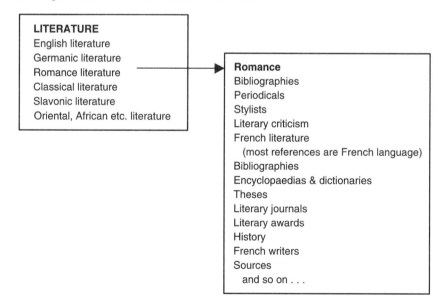

Figure 2.3 *Consulting reference sources: Walford on 'romantic literature'*

Given that the scope of the topic has been initially defined like this –

Topic: French romance literature
Limits: English and French language materials
Exclude: poetry and drama

– the list of source types might look like this:

Romance

Types of sources	**Information requirements**
• Bibliographies	List of general bibliographies that index French romance and of specific bibliographies on French romance
• Abstracts and indexes	List of relevant abstracts and indexes covering French romance
• Periodicals	List of core periodicals that publish on romance
• Stylists	List of reference sources on stylists, especially bibliographies
• Abstracts on literary criticism	List of general and specific abstracts that index literary critical works on French romance literature
• Encyclopaedias and dictionaries	List of general works on literature and list of specific works on romance literature
• Theses	List abstracts that index PhD theses
• Literary awards	List of literary awards for romance writing
• History	Texts and bibliographies on the history of romance
• Writers	List of key romance writers and their work
• Libraries with romance holdings	List of directories of libraries and other sources that stock romance literature
• Publishers	List of directories of publishers associated with romance publications

Tip: *use Appendix 4 for guidance on how to cite your references.*

In summary, a literature search requires planning. By consulting guides to the literature, lists of relevant sources can be constructed. From these and the reference sources described in this book a systematic search can be undertaken. The time and effort spent planning the search will be rewarded: all possible sources will have been listed and, if followed through, you should have the knowledge of a job well done.

SUMMARY OF THIS CHAPTER

1 Plan the search before you begin – it will save time and help you organize your tasks.
2 Use the materials in the quick reference section of the library to define the parameters of your search.
3 Use guides to the literature to identify useful abstracts and indexes and other sources.
4 Set up a system to manage your notes, especially the construction of bibliographies.

3

Search management

This chapter will show you how:

- to maintain a record of your search – a *search log*
- to learn from your experience to improve your searching technique
- to manage your time effectively and efficiently
- to cite references

It cannot be over-emphasized that strict management of the search is an essential part of the search for literature relevant to your topic. Keeping *accurate*, *consistent* and *correct* records is the basis of good project management. Figure 3.1 shows some of the main elements for managing the massive amount of information that a literature search generates.

KEEPING A LOG OF YOUR SEARCH

A search log has three main functions:

- to act as a *record* of your activities during your search of the literature;
- to act as *data* for your dissertation;
- to act as a *learning resource*.

First, your log should *record* what you did, when and where, with what, and what the results were, and what follow-up actions need to be taken to complete a task. As *data* your log should be the basis for writing up how you did your search of the literature, providing a clear description of what you did. This is so that you can show, in your dissertation or thesis, that your search was systematic and comprehensive. As a *learning resource* your log can be the basis for improving your knowledge and understanding of the principles and concepts of how information is stored, organized and can be retrieved.

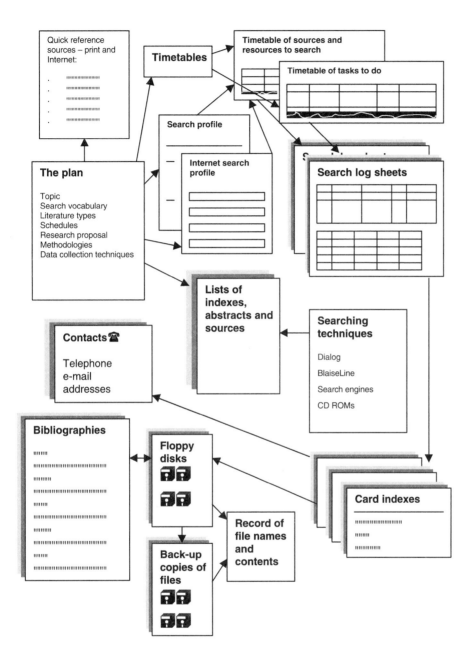

Figure 3.1 *Diverse elements for managing a literature search*

Table 3.1   *Suggested sections for a literature search log*

Section in your file	Contents
1 Plan	Your plan that you developed using Chapter 2, especially Figure 2.1, and the quick reference section of the library.
2 Timetable	A weekly schedule of what resources and sources you intend to look at and search beginning with the pre-search planning stage (see Table 3.3).
3 Search profile sheets	Your search sheets with details of your search parameters and search vocabulary as suggested in Appendix 3, 'Literature search profile' and Appendix 9, 'Internet search profile'.
4 Search log sheets	Sheets recording what you searched, when and how, and what results were obtained (see Table 3.2).
5 Bibliographies	Bibliographies for all the sub-sections of your topic. Remember to have copies of these in another location in case you lose your file.
6 Contact details	A list of useful contacts including the phone number of your university subject librarian and tutor.
7 Discussion groups	Notes on relevant discussion lists and news forums that you can use.
8 Inter-library loans	A running log of what you have read, made copies of and ordered from the inter-library loans service of your library.
9 CD ROMs, online databases and Internet sources	A list of the primary and secondary sources and resources that you have identified as needing to be searched.
10 Search techniques	Notes on searching different databases, especially the use of Boolean logic.
11 File names	List of file names on your floppy disks and computer.
12 Miscellaneous	E.g. style sheets for citations, new web sites to visit.
13 Reminders	Daily or weekly reminders of things to do, especially your project housekeeping.

How to keep a search log

Using a simple ring binder make notes and file them appropriately on the activities of your literature search. Table 3.1 gives some suggestions on what records you should keep in your search log. Remember that the records of your literature search will normally form a part of your overall *research diary*.

It is important that the search log is a contemporaneous record of your search. This means it needs to be started during the planning stages of your literature search and every time you do something on your search it needs to be recorded.

Tip: *do not spend time on excessive presentation in your log – it only wastes time and effort.*

Nothing in the log should be thrown away until some time after you have completed your research, written your project and had a successful outcome to your research, e.g. been awarded your Master's or Doctorate. Do not try to produce perfect records using a word processor and computer databases. Handwritten notes are perfectly adequate so long as they are clear, up to date and well organized.

Some of the suggestions in Table 3.1 are self-explanatory but some need further description and illustration and we will look at these now.

CONSTRUCTING A BIBLIOGRAPHY

There are various methods you can use to construct and maintain a bibliography. The manual method amounts to establishing a card index with each item being indexed on to one or more cards. The cards are then arranged in some logical order, say, alphabetically. However, given the massive amount of literature available, many researchers use electronic means to store, organize and retrieve citations. There are a number of ways a personal computer can be used to create a personal bibliography. In practice it is easier to record bibliographic items first on cards and then to transfer these to a personal computer.

> **Tip:** *print-outs from downloads of citations can be cut up and pasted on to cards.*

Card index

A simple card index for book materials might look like this:

```
AUTHOR                          Date

Title
Place of publication
Publisher
Notes
```

Electronic databases

A range of software for constructing bibliographies is widely available. Some people adapt word-processing packages, while others invest in dedicated software. Even the most simple of word-processing packages can provide a means to produce lists of items the can be regularly updated. The more sophisticated packages enable the researcher to print selections of records in a variety of formats for different document types. One of the most popular commercial bibliographical packages is ProCite, from CiteWise.com (a division of Cherwell Scientific).

The key advantages of electronic databases are that:

- you can extract bibliographical records in a variety of pre-determined formats to suit different needs, e.g. the different requirements of different journals;

- you can search the bibliography using key words;
- you can automatically arrange the items according to different criteria, e.g. date of publication, by author or by key word;
- you can check the spelling of author names and titles in your text;
- you can add notes to (annotate) the record;
- you can download data from CD ROM and online databases into the bibliography;
- you can make automatic changes to the typography to meet the needs of different journal styles;
- you can edit records easily and transfer them to other parts of the database;
- you can copy all or part of the database to create a card index that you can carry with you when you need to check something, say in the library.

Whatever system you use, keeping a log of what you have done and need to do is important. When you are in the library a simple manual log, as indicated in Table 3.2, will be sufficient.

Citing references and attribution

You must keep full bibliographical details of items you find during your search. As you will probably have several sub-topics within your general topic this means using your card index to construct several bibliographies in which some of the cards will be duplicates. Record the full bibliographical details of items that you have identified as relevant. The alternative is to try and remember the details, which is impossible, especially when you are likely to have 50–70 references for an undergraduate project and many more for a postgraduate dissertation or thesis. In Appendix 4, 'How to cite sources', you will find suggestions on how to cite references for a range of material including the Internet, but for further advice and updates see web sites such as the following, which give links to the major sources on how to cite materials:

- **Librarian's index to the Internet**
  (address – http://lii.org/)
- **The world wide web virtual library**
  (address – www.spaceless.com/WWWVL/)

The full citation of other people's work is essential: this is known as *attribution* – the scholarly standard of acknowledging where ideas in your own work have their origins. Not only is it unethical to use someone else's work without referencing it but it can be an infringement of copyright to do so. Therefore make a record of the bibliographical details of work you consider relevant to your topic to ensure that you acknowledge the work of others that you use in your own research.

Table 3.2 Extract from a search log: bibliographical details

Source	Search terms	Dates to search + hits	Dates/Time	Notes
Sociofile	'literature searching'	1990✓2 91✓3 92✓0 93✓4 94✓2 95✓1 96✓2 97✓5 98✓5 99✓7 00✓3 Total = 34	25/3/00 2 hrs	Peters = main author on lit searching? Check citation indexes.

Year	Hit Number	Author	Get copy	In library	ILL ordered
1990	2	Jones	Yes	yes	
1991	1	Peters	Yes	yes	
1993	3	Peters	Yes	no	yes 25/3/00
1994	2	Barns	Yes	no	yes 25/3/00

Note the bibliographical details of these selected results and add them to your bibliography.
Note on your bibliography if your have read or got a copy of the article or when one was
ordered from inter-library loan (ILL) so that you can keep a check of articles received.

Add to your list of things to do.

Maintain your housekeeping

Organizing your notes and managing your project is part of the general housekeeping of a literature search. General but essential housekeeping also involves the following routine tasks:

Set up a physical filing system   Use a physical store to keep and index articles and copies of materials that you have made. You will collect many of these during your search. It is important to index and write an abstract for each of them and file them so that they can be retrieved when you need them.

Set up files on your computer   Create and give consecutive file names to your bibliographies and working notes, and place these into directories on your computer. Put each bibliography on a separate disk to avoid over-writing and the loss of your data. Do not use an obscure software application but stick to common applications. Make a record in your search log of the names and content of your files and remember to delete files you do not need to avoid having multiple versions of a file on your computer and disks.

Make back-up files of your computer files   At least once each week make back-up copies of all your files and keep these in a safe place. As well as making copies of your files on to other floppy disks you can send them via e-mail to a friend who has consented to store your copies on their machine. You can do this by incorporating the file-back-up task into your timetable of tasks to be done. All too often disks are lost or damaged, and with a back-up you will avoid retracing work you have already done.

Do printouts of your computer files   As well as making copies of all your files, after each time you work on a file do a printout of that file. Although this can be time consuming, if by some chance a disaster does strike and you lose all your files, including the back-ups, at least you will have a hard copy to work from. Regular printouts will also give you material you can carry around with you to examine and analyse when you get the time.

USING INDEXES AND ABSTRACTS

Using indexes and abstracts is a relatively simple task. Once you understand the basic principles of how they are arranged then with practice you should become a proficient user of any indexing and abstracting service and skilled in writing your own abstracts of materials you find.

Using indexing services

The main difference between an abstract and an index is that indexes do not contain summaries of the work. Indexes arrange entries under subject headings and sometimes under author names. Many indexes provide lists of headings under which entries have been arranged. These are worth looking at because not all relevant work will have been entered under the same heading. Headings used by an indexing service also help you to expand or narrow the field of your search. An index will give the bibliographical details of a publication, so an indexing service that provides abstracts can be far more useful for determining the relevance of a hit.

Using abstracting services

Abstracting publications tend to concentrate on a particular subject area such as sociology (*Sociological Abstracts*) or psychology (*Psychological Abstracts*). The example in Figure 3.2 is taken from the SocioFile CD ROM (*Sociological Abstracts*) and shows some of the main features of a good abstracting service.

Annotating and writing abstracts

There are two main types of abstract, *informative* and *indicative*. An informative abstract provides a summary of the principal arguments and data of the original document. An indicative abstract provides a short summary of the intention of the author while allowing the reader to decide whether it is worth obtaining the full article to read. Consulting abstracts provided by the indexing services can be an efficient use of time when deciding which items should be read and which need only to be noted.

> **Tip:** when writing an abstract provide information on who did what, when and how, and what they found or argued.

Reading abstracts often gives a good idea on how to write them. The informative abstract usually has the same structure as the original document and normally includes the following:

- Purpose   The purpose of the research; what the author was attempting to achieve (aims). The abstract will normally use words and phrases from the original document.
- Method   The method(s) used to do the research will be listed. Only brief details will be provided because it is assumed that the reader knows about methods and methodology.
- Results   A key phrase or sentence provides brief information on the results of the research. There is no assessment of those results that the reader of the abstract can use to judge the relevance of the original document.

	Record 1 of 1 - Sociofile (1/74 - 8/92)
Title	TI: Stereotypes of Mental Illness: A Test of the Labelling Hypothesis
Authors	AU: Jones,-Lizanne; Cochrane,-Raymond
Institution	IN: U Birmingham, B15 2TT England
Journal	JN: International-Journal-of-Social-Psychiatry; 1981, 27, 2, summer, 99-107.
	AVA: Hard copy reproduction not available; document not on microfilm
	DT: aja Abstract-of-Journal-Article
Language	LA: English
Country of publication	CP: United Kingdom
Date published	PY: 1981
Abstract	AB: To examine the existence of mental illness stereotypes, a questionnaire was administered to 82 M & 51 F Coll students. Data support the following conclusions: (1) mental illness stereotypes do exist & closely resemble the behavior of psychiatric patients described in objective studies; (2) such stereotypes are not necessarily sex-differentiated, & some of the perceived differences between mentally ill Fs & Ms are attributable to normal sex-role differentiation; & (3) the stereotypes of a 'normal' & a mentally ill F correlate quite closely, but M stereotypes do not. 1 Table, 31 References. Modified HA (Copyright 1985, Sociological Abstracts, Inc., all rights reserved.)
Terms used for indexing	DE: Mental-illness, Mentally-ill (267175); Stereotype, Stereotypes, Stereotyped, Stereotyping (445000)
	IP: mental illness stereotypes; questionnaire; college students;
	SH: sociology of health and medicine; sociology of medicine (public health) (2046)
Identification numbers	CC: 2046; 2000
	AN: 8505541

(Adapted from Sociofile SilverPlatter CD-ROM)

Figure 3.2   *An abstract*

The indicative abstract does not always follow the structure of the original document. It attempts to provide some guidance on the value of the document to our understanding of the topic. The indicative abstract usually provides a summary of the contents in a sentence or two and a brief assessment of the document. This can be an outline of the argument its author makes or the contribution the document has made to the understanding of an issue or topic. The usefulness of references or material that has been appended may also be mentioned.

In Figure 3.2 you should be able to see several essential pieces of information that you can use for your own records and searching. These include:

- bibliographical details for your own bibliography,
  - author(s)
  - title
  - journal title
  - date of publication
  - number of pages;
- contacts – the authors;
- terms used for indexing – check to see if these are included on your search term list (search vocabulary);
- details in the abstract.

USING THE SEARCH LOG AS A LEARNING EXERCISE

Your search log can be more than a record of what you did; it can also be an opportunity for you to learn new skills. One way to think about your search of the literature is to see it as giving you an understanding that you can use to improve your capabilities the next time you have an information-seeking and information-management job to do. The model of learning shown in Figure 3.3 is derived from Kolb, Rubin and MacIntyre

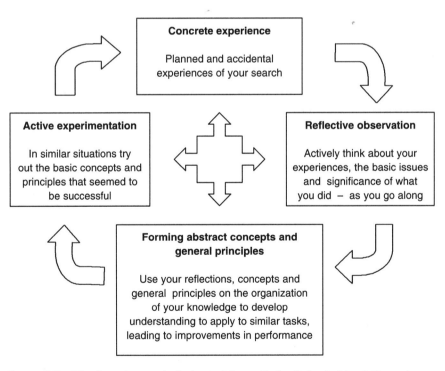

Figure 3.3   *The learning cycle (adapted from Kolb, D.A., Rubin, I.M. and MacIntyre, J.M., Organizational psychology, 4th edn. London: Prentice Hall, 1984)*

(1984) and shows how you can use your literature search as an active way of learning by reflecting on your experience and adapting it for use in similar situations.

TIME MANAGEMENT

Time is a very scare and therefore a valuable resource. Your plan can help you to use time effectively and efficiently. With a time-table, plan your activities and base them on the notion of *sessions* that are broken down into *tasks* to be done. Your timetable should be based on your plan for your literature search; Table 3.3 shows an extract from a search timetable. Once you have identified which sources and resources *need* to be searched, then allocate sufficient time in terms of sessions to search each in a logical order.

> **Tip:** *learn how long a search of an individual source takes as you go along and adjust your timetable accordingly after your first few sessions.*

Here are seven tips to help you use your time efficiently

1 Know what you want to search before you go to the library or turn on your computer. This will direct your efforts to the tasks that *need* to be done.
2 Book CD ROMs, a computer and any other resource in the library in advance.
3 If using a computer, use the one hour on, one hour off, one hour on format. Use your hour off the machine to organize your notes, reflect on what still needs to be done and how you can do better with the remaining hour. Remember to take short breaks from a computer to rest your eyes and stretch your muscles.
4 Go equipped with pencils, pens and paper, and your search profile sheets.
5 Stick to your search plan, working on one thing at a time. If you need to deviate from your plan make a note of why, and if possible book an additional session.
6 Do not devote effort to not doing things. Chatting to others, staring out the window and doodling are task-displacement activities and therefore only waste valuable time.
7 If you smoke, give up: it wastes time and might damage your health.

Table 3.3 *Extract from a search timetable*

Source	Format	Place	Time	Booked	Search terms
Sociofile	CD ROM	University	Wed 25/3 PM	1.30–2.30/ 3.30–4.30	'literature searching'
Soc SciSearch	Dialog	University	Thur 26/3 AM	9.30–10.30	'literature searching'

There are plenty of books that can give you further advice on managing your time. These include the following:

- **Better time management**.
  Atkinson, J. London: Kogan Page, 1992. 📖
- **First things first: how to manage your time for maximum performance**.
  Forsyth, P. London: Institute of Management/Pitman, 1994. 📖

SUMMARY OF THIS CHAPTER

1 Set up your management system in advance of starting your search of the literature.
2 Keep accurate, consistent and clear records of what you did, when, and the results.
3 Use timetables and forward planning to organize the use of your time.
4 Learn as you go along and try to reflect on how to improve your searching techniques.

Part B

LITERATURE TYPES: WORKING THROUGH THE BIBLIOGRAPHICAL FRAMEWORK

Quick reference materials

This chapter will show you:

- how to use guides to the literature to identify dictionaries, encyclopaedias, biographies, yearbooks, directories and other reference materials
- what reference materials can do to help you define your topic and construct a search vocabulary

All academic libraries stock a standard range of materials in the quick reference section. Here you will find reference sources such as guides to the literature, dictionaries, encyclopaedias, yearbooks and directories. The quick reference section is therefore essential to any research project. It can introduce you to a new subject area, clarify a subject by providing citations, provide a vocabulary for further searching, and provide key facts and figures. Figure 4.1 is a route map to this chapter: in the subsections that follow you will find more detailed information on the sources shown in the figure.

DICTIONARIES

There are three main types of dictionary: *general language dictionaries*, which give definitions of words and phrases and sometimes the origins of words; *subject dictionaries*, which provide definitions of terms relating to specific subjects; and *biographical* dictionaries, which provide information on people living and dead. Following in the next section is a list of dictionaries that most university libraries and larger public libraries will have in their quick reference section. Remember that some are available on CD ROM, and among these are 'talking' dictionaries.

Tip: *for a list of some subject dictionaries see Appendix 5.*

Finding dictionaries

To see if there is a dictionary on your subject area consult references such as the following:

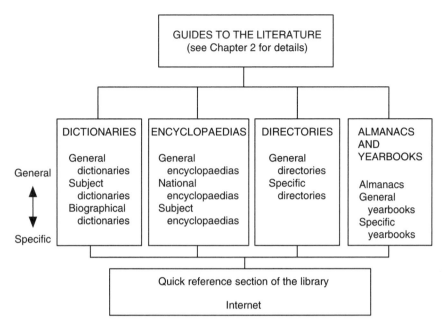

Figure 4.1 *Examples of sources to be found in the quick reference section*

- **Dictionary of dictionaries**.
  Kabdebo, T. and Armstrong, N. London: Bowker-Saur, 1997. A good one-volume guide to dictionaries and encyclopaedias. 📖
- **Caltech general reference page**.
  (address – http://library.caltech.edu/reference/default.htm).
  Useful set of links to a range of reference sources including encyclopaedias and dictionaries such as a hypertext *Webster's dictionary*. 🕸
- **A web of online dictionaries**.
  (address – www.facstaff.bucknell.edu/rbeard/diction.html).
  Beard, R. 1996. This will search over 800 dictionaries, including etymological dictionaries, and thesauri in 150 languages, with preference given to free online sources. 🕸
- **Roget's thesaurus**.
  (address – http://humanities.uchicago.edu/forms_unrest/ROGET. html).
  From the University of Chicago, key word or full text can be searched with clickable hypertext links. 📖 🕸
- **BUBL Link**.
  (address – http://bubl.ac.uk/types/dictionaries.html).
  Bubl link lists over 140 dictionaries and related sources. 🕸
- **HUMBUL: Online dictionary**.
  (address – http://firth.oucs.ox.ac.uk/).
  Provides an online dictionary search with links to many other reference sources.

General language dictionaries

A good print dictionary is an invaluable resource for all researchers. Here are some popular titles, but remember to check for new editions.

- **Oxford English dictionary**.
  On disc and in printed forms, 20 vols. Oxford: Oxford University Press, 1989. This is the most comprehensive and detailed English language dictionary. It provides information on the origins (etymology) of words. Very useful for tracing how the use and meaning of a word have changed. 📖 ☉
- **Klien's comprehensive etymological dictionary of the English language**.
  2 vols. Klien, E. Amsterdam: Elsevier, 1965–76. Over 45,000 entries giving full etymological analysis of terms, tracing their introduction into the English language. 📖
- **Origins**.
  Partridge, E. London: Routledge, 1990. An etymological dictionary of modern English. 📖

Other dictionaries that can normally be found in the quick reference section, in bookshops and on the Internet include the following:

- **Webster's third new international dictionary of the British language**.
  3 vols. Chicago: Encyclopaedia Britannica, 1986. 📖
- **Hypertext Webster interface dictionary and thesaurus**.
  (address – http://c.gp.cs.cmu.edu:5103/prog/webster/). 🕸
- **Collins dictionary of the English language**.
  London: Collins, 1979. 📖
- **The concise Oxford dictionary of current English**.
  8th edn. Oxford: Clarendon Press, 1990. 📖

General dictionaries for social science

> **Tip:** *always have a good general dictionary, thesaurus and social science dictionary handy.*

There are a number of dictionaries that provide good overviews of ideas, theories and concepts in social science. Consult the following when researching any topic within the social sciences, humanities and arts:

- **The Fontana dictionary of modern social thought**.
  Bollock, A. London: Fontana Press, 1988. 📖
- **A new dictionary of the social sciences**.
  2nd edn. Aldine Publishing, 1980. 📖
- **Dictionary of the social sciences**.
  Gould, J. and Kolb, W.K. London: Tavistock Publications for UNESCO, 1964. 📖

- **The Blackwell dictionary of twentieth century social thought**.
  Outhewaite, W. and Bottomore, T. (eds). Oxford: Blackwell, 1993. 📖
- **Dictionary of the history of ideas: studies of selected pivotal ideas**.
  5 vols. Weiner, P.P. (ed.). New York: Scribner's, 1980. 📖
- **The Oxford companion to the mind**.
  Gregory, R.L. and Zangwill, O.L. (eds). Oxford: Oxford University Press, 1988. 📖

There are also some dictionaries on methodology in the social sciences including:

- **A dictionary of social science methods**.
  MacMiller, P. and Wilson, M.J. Chichester: Wiley, 1983. 📖
- **Dictionary of statistics and methodology: a non-technical guide for the social sciences**.
  2nd edn. Vogt, W.P. London: Sage Publications, 1998. 📖

Subject dictionaries

Many of the individual disciplines have dictionaries that deal with subject-specific terms, concepts and the theorists. There are hundreds of specific dictionaries. Look out for some of the more unusual, such as *The city, a dictionary of quotable thought on cities and urban life*, by J.A. Clapp. New Brunswick, NJ: Center for Urban Policy Research, 1984. Remember that many of these have bibliographies and are indexed.

> **Tip:** *use a selection of subject dictionaries to build up different definitions and usages of words and concepts.*

Biographical dictionaries and sources

Knowing something about the historical context in which authors produced their work can be useful. Knowing who is who, or who was who, and what they did can provide material essential to constructing a map of authorities in a subject area. There is a very wide range of reference sources that provide an incredible amount of information on thousands of people. Biographical sources will also answer such questions as, 'How do you spell A's name?' and 'When did Y die?' Many biographical dictionaries provide this along with references to works by particular authors. There are three broad categories of biographical dictionary: *general biographies*, containing entries of persons from all countries and times; *national biographies*, containing entries of persons from specific countries or regions; and *specialized biographies*, containing entries on persons with a specific association or from a certain subject area. As a general rule most subjects, countries and professions have biographical works dedicated to them.

Finding a biographical source A variety of publications provides surveys and contents listings of biographies. Some of these guides, however, often refer to obscure publications that may be difficult to obtain. Nevertheless these and other guides can save you time and effort by identifying relevant and obtainable biographical works:

- **Biography almanac.**
  2nd edn. Stetler, S. (ed.). Detroit: Gale, 1983. This is a guide to about 20,000 'prominent' individuals from biblical times to the present who have appeared in 325 biographical dictionaries. 📖
- **A dictionary of universal biography of all ages and all peoples.**
  2nd edn. Hyamson, A.M. London: Routledge, 1951. This contains references to about 100,000 biographies appearing in 24 major biographical dictionaries. 📖
- **International bibliography of biography 1970–87.**
  12 vols. London: Bowker-Saur, 1988. This contains references to 56,000 biographies. 📖
- **ARBA guide to biographical resources, 1986–1996.**
  Wick, R.L. (ed.). London: Libraries Unlimited, 1996. 📖

In addition, some large multi-directory web sites and online sources have substantial biographical information. These include the following:

- **Biographical resource centre.**
  Gale Research. Over 50 databases, many previously available in print, combined with 900,000 thumbnail biographies from *Who's Who* (includes some images). ☎
- **Wilson biography mega.**
  Wilson. Online access to many biographical sources (includes some images). ☎
- **BUBL Link: biography.**
  (address – http://bubl.ac.uk/link/types/biographies.html and http://bubl.ac.uk:80/biography.html). 🕸
  Provides access to many biographical sources and biographies.

General biographical sources
- **Webster's new biographical dictionary.**
  Springfield, MA: Merriam, 1988. Contains about 40,000 short biographies providing information on nationality, occupation and achievements. 📖
- **The McGraw-Hill encyclopaedia of world biography.**
  12 vols. New York and London: McGraw-Hill, 1975. Very broad in coverage, containing current, retrospective and subject-based biographies. 📖
- **Macmillan dictionary of biography.**
  2nd edn. Jones, B. and Dixon, M.V. London: Macmillan, 1985. Focuses on contemporaries and provides bibliographies with cross-references. 📖

- **Current biography**.
  Wilson. Monthly with annual culmination, 1940. This provides lively material on about 350 celebrities from the arts, sport, entertainment and government. Recent photographs are included, as well as personal information not usually found elsewhere. 📖
- **New York Times biographical service**.
  Ann Arbor: University of Michigan, Micofilms International. Monthly in print and available through NEXIS Online. Provides about 150 photo-copied articles, interviews and obituaries from the newspaper. 📖 ☎
- **Who's who**.
  Annual since 1849. London: Black. Contains about 30,000 biographical sketches. There are many similar titles, including *Who's who in France; Who's who in Germany; Who's who in America* and many others. 📖 ⊙
- **The Cambridge biographical encyclopaedia**.
  (address – www.biography.com/find.html).
  Details on 20,000 individuals with cross-referencing. 🏛

General retrospective biographies
- **Dictionary of national biography**.
  63 vols. London: Smith Elder. 1885–1901; reissue: 2 vols, 1908-09; 2nd to 10th supplements, 1901–85; and Oxford: Oxford University Press, 1912–90. An incredible reference source of lengthy articles researched from a wide range of sources. Includes bibliographies with the entries. 📖
- **British biographical archive**.
  Munich: Bowker-Saur, 1984. Microfiche archive of about 200,000 records on individuals. Records have been collected from English language references dating from 1601 to 1929. 📖

Subject-specific biographical sources There are many subject-specific biographical sources covering a very wide range of topics, including portraits, writers, politicians, scientists and other persons from many fields of study and

> **Tip:** *many encyclopaedias provide biographical information on major theorists.*

art. Here is a selection of some interesting subject-specific biographical sources available via the Internet and in print:

- **Bjorn's guide to philosophy**.
  (address – www.knuten.liu.se/~bjoch509/). 🏛
- **Distinguished women of past and present**.
  (address – www.netsrq.com/~dbois/index.html). 🏛
- **Dead sociologists index**.
  (address – http://diogenes.baylor.edu/WWWproviders/Larry_Rid-ener/DSS/INDEX.html). 🏛
- **Biographical dictionary of psychology**.
  Sheehy, N., Chapman, A.J. and Conroy, W. (eds). London: Routledge, 1997. 📖

- **Biographical dictionary of twentieth century philosophers**.
  Brown, S., Collinson, D. and Wilkinson, R. (eds). London: Routledge, 1995. 📖
- **A–Z guide to modern social and political theorists**.
  Sim, S. and Parker, N. London: Prentice-Hall, 1997. 📖

ENCYCLOPAEDIAS

The main difference between an encyclopaedia and a dictionary is that a dictionary attempts to define whereas an encyclopaedia attempts to describe by putting a term into context. The distinction, however, is not always clear cut. For example, *The encyclopaedic dictionary of psychology*, by Harry, R. and Lamb, R. (Oxford: Blackwell, 1983) is part dictionary and part encyclopaedia.

> **Tip:** *some CD ROM encyclopaedias give links to web sites (hyperlinks).*

Some general encyclopaedias are very expensive, for example the *Encyclopaedia Britannica*, and should therefore only be consulted in the library. Some subject encyclopaedias can be very useful and cost effective, e.g. the *Blackwell dictionary of twentieth century social thought* (1993). Generally the more recent the encyclopaedia the more current will be its contents. However, do not overlook some of the older publications especially if looking at older ideas and theories. One that is early, yet very useful, is the *Encyclopaedia of the social sciences, 1930–1935*, edited by Seligman, E.R.A. and Johnson, A.S. (New York: Macmillan, 1935).

> **Tip:** *for a list of some subject-specific encyclopaedias see Appendix 6.*

> **Tip:** *we have used the British spelling, 'encyclopaedia'. The US spelling is encyclopedia.*

Finding encyclopaedias

To see if there is an encyclopaedia on your subject area consult references such as the following:

- **Dictionary of dictionaries and eminent encyclopaedias: comprising dictionaries, encyclopaedias and other selected wordbooks in English**.
  2nd edn. Kabdebo, T. and Armstrong, N. London: Bowker-Saur, 1997. 📖
- **Guide to subject encyclopaedias: user guide, review citations and key word index**.
  Mirwis, A. Phoenix, AZ: Oryx Press (dist. UK Eurospan, London), 1998.
- **Acses**.
  (address – www.acses.com/).
  Web service that searches the catalogues of most publishers for items still available. 🕸

- **BUBL Link**.
  (address – http://bubl.ac.uk/reference/).
  Provides a list of encyclopaedias and related sources. ⬟

General-purpose encyclopaedias

- **Encyclopaedia Britannica CD 99 multimedia edition**.
  32 vols. An enormous encyclopaedia and the most famous, it is divided
  into four sections: 📖 ☉ ⬟
    - Propaedia (gives an outline of knowledge)
    - Micropaedia (quick ready reference to articles)
    - Macropaedia (knowledge in-depth)
    - indexes (cross-reference index)
- **The new Grolier multimedia encyclopedia**.
  CD ROM version of the 21-volume *Academic American Encyclopaedia*. ☉
- **Encyclopedia Americana**.
  CD ROM 30 vols. Danbury, CT: American Corp., 1995. ☉
- **Encarta** – *The CD ROM Microsoft Encarta encyclopaedia: world English
  edition*.
  Designed from the outset to be an electronic reference work, includes
  video, animation, images and links to web sites (hyperlinks). ☉
- **Encyclopaedia.com**.
  (address – www.encyclopaedia.com/).
  Free online encyclopaedia based on the *Concise Columbia Electronic
  Encyclopaedia*, 3rd edn. Links to graphics and articles are fee based. ⬟

General encyclopaedias for the social sciences

Good subject-based encyclopaedias can be very useful for a range of
scholarly tasks. Ideas and theories you come across can be looked up, the
names of people checked, key publications on a topic identified and
biographical information obtained, along with dates and some statistics.
Here is a selection of useful general encyclopaedias, in the social sciences:

- **The Blackwell dictionary of twentieth century social thought**.
  1 vol. Outhewaite, W. and Bottomore, T. (eds). Oxford: Blackwell, 1993.
  Part dictionary, part encyclopaedia that includes biographical
  information on social theorists. Has long and detailed entries that
  give the history of many ideas and theories and provide further
  readings. Most entries are written by authorities in the field yet are
  easy to understand. It covers most disciplines in the social sciences,
  with good coverage of ideas and social movements. 📖
- **International encyclopedia of the social sciences**.
  17 vols. Sills, D.L. (ed.). New York: Macmillan and Free Press, 1979.
  Biographical supplement, 1979. A scholarly work with entries written by
  relevant social scientists. It has very wide coverage including geography

and history but not education. It concentrates on the analytical, comparative and contemporary rather than the etymological and has substantial bibliographies and an excellent index to the 1,716 articles. ▣

- **Encyclopedia plus: encyclopedia of world problems and human potential**.
  CD ROM Bowker-Saur. Details of 12,000 issues – social, economic and political with 250,000 hyperlinks. ⊙
- **The encyclopaedia mythica**.
  (address – www.pantheon.org/mythica/)
  Covers mythology, folklore and mysticism, with thousands of articles and bibliographical sources. ✿
- **The social science encyclopaedia**.
  Kuper, A. and Kuper, J. (eds). London: Routledge, 1999.
- **Encyclopaedia of contemporary British culture**.
  London: Routledge, 1999. ▣
- **Stanford encyclopedia of philosophy**.
  (address – http://plato.stanford.edu/). Searchable encyclopaedia based on submitted articles. ✿
- **Women in world history**.
  (address – www.galegroup.com/).
  A biographical encyclopaedia with over 8,000 entries and 1,500 articles of up to 5,000 words in length.

Remember that other publications, such as *History of humanity*, 5 vols (London: Routledge, in association with UNESCO, 1999), can fill gaps in your knowledge of world history and culture.

DIRECTORIES, ALMANACS AND YEARBOOKS

In order to find the names and addresses of potentially useful organizations and associations you can consult a directory. Yearbooks and manuals also contain useful information, often about the organization, e.g. if it has a library. The kinds of questions that these sources can answer are, 'How many people live in Norway?', 'Who is the President of the European Union?' and 'What is the defence budget of the UK?'

Definition: *Almanac* and *yearbook*

Almanacs provide a compendium of useful current, retrospective and comparative data and information on countries, people, places, events, subjects, etc.

Yearbooks provide an annual compendium of data and information for a given year.

Finding directories

To find out if a directory or yearbook exists that may be of help to your research consult the following:

- **Current British directories**.
  Beckenham: CBD Research, 1999. A guide to research directories published in the British Isles. Regularly updated, this has a wide scope and includes references to registers, membership lists, and *Who's who*. 📖
- **Directory of directories**.
  Detroit: Gale Research, 1999. An annotated guide to over 9,600 business and industrial directories from North America. 📖 ⊙
- **Directories in print**.
  Detroit: Gale Research, 1999. Describes approximately 15,500 guides. 📖 ⊙
- **BUBL Link: directories**.
  (address – http://bubl.ac.uk/link/types/directories.html).
  Access to over 86 directories and related sources. 🕸
- **Gale directory of databases**.
  Detroit: Gale Research, 1999. Comprehensive coverage of over 12,500 databases available worldwide. 📖 ⊙

Some examples of common directories are:

- **Directory of British associations**.
  CBD Research, 1998. Regular updates. 📖
- **Social services yearbook**.
  Harlow: Longman, 1996. Regular updates. 📖
- **Guide to the social services**.
  London: Family Welfare Association, 1995. 📖
- **Directory of social research organizations in the UK**.
  Sykes, B.S. (ed.). London: Mansell, 1998. Regular updates. 📖
- **NameFLOW-paradise service**.
  (address – www.dante.net/nameflow.html). 🕸
  This gives access to over a million people and thousands of organizations across the world. 🕸

Almanacs and yearbooks

These two types of source will provide you with facts and information on people, places, events and many more subjects, allowing you to make comparisons and identify trends as well as other sources of information. Some common sources in the category include:

> **Tip:** *some almanacs, yearbooks and fact books are available online.*

- **Whitaker's almanack**.
  London: J. Whitaker & Sons, 1869 to date. 📖 ☎
- **Year book plus**.
  London: Bowker-Saur. Annual updates with links to many web sites.
  ⊙ 📖
- **The CIA world factbook**.
  London: HMSO. (address – http://www.odci.gov/cia/publications/factbook/index.html). 🕸
- **International historical statistics**.
  3 vols. Mitchell, B.R. London: Macmillan, 1998. 📖
- **Ready reference collection of the Internet public library**.
  (address – http://www.ipl.org/ref/RR/static/ref0000.html). 🕸
  Includes links to almanacs, biographies, encyclopaedias, geographical information and other facts.
- **Keesing's record of world events**.
  Keesing's Worldwide. 1960 to the present day. Information on elections, people, wars, trends, organizations and more. ⊙ 🕸

ONE-STOP REFERENCE RESOURCES

There is also a range of one-stop services which incorporates directories, almanacs and yearbooks along with other factual sources. Some of these are:

- **KnowUK**.
  (address – www.knowuk.co.uk/).
  Provides information on people, places, institutions, governments and events. 🕸
- **The Nutshell**.
  (address – www.thenutshell.co.uk/).
  London: Bowker-Saur. Aimed at the information specialist but with references to electronic journals, events, news and abstracts. 🕸
- **Gale's ready reference shelf**.
  Detroit: Gale Research. Multi-volume reference collection on organizations, associations, research centres and databases. ⊙
- **Infoplease.com**.
  (address – www.infoplease.com/).
  Web search service that gives access to some dictionaries, encyclopaedias, almanacs and other reference sources. 🕸
- **Mediaeater reference desk**.
  (address – www.mediaeater.com/).
  Provides links to a large number of reference sources including dictionaries, atlases and fact books. 🕸
- **Research it!**
  (address – www.iTools.com/).

Provides access to several diverse reference sources including language translators. 🏯

- **Librarian's resource centre**.
  (address – www.sla.org/).
  A selective collection of links to reference materials.

SUMMARY OF THIS CHAPTER

- There are many different kinds of reference sources that can help you refine your topic – some are invaluable to the researcher.
- Use general and subject dictionaries to build up different definitions of a term or concept.
- Encyclopaedias will give you an overview of a topic and provide some initial references – many will be key texts – and some CD ROM encyclopaedias give hyperlinks.
- Biographical sources can give you key publications for theorists and researchers.
- Directories, almanacs and yearbooks will provide facts on people, places and events.

5

Finding books and bibliographies

This chapter will show you:

- how to locate books on your topic
- how to find electronic books
- how to find bibliographies relevant to your topic
- how to use libraries, especially the British Library

Books and articles are the sources of material most sought after by researchers. Typically the search for books begins with a search of the library OPAC (Online Public Access Catalogue). Once this has been done you can move on to search bibliographies such as the *British National Bibliography* as well as the OPACs from other libraries. The point to note is that the search for books is not a discrete phase: it continues throughout the literature search. The typical types of sources to be searched are shown in Figure 5.1.

Tip: *you can search the OPACs of many libraries via the Internet along with catalogues of the British Library using gateways such as NISS and BUBL.*

Tip: *see Chapter 2 for criteria that can help you find core texts.*

Figure 5.1 also shows the chronology of published materials, from books published in the past to books recently published and to books planned. If the scope of the search is to find all relevant book material then the aim is to locate past publications as well as recent publications. This will include aiming to locate seminal and core texts (work that has had a major influence on a topic) in the literature of a topic. Using a core text the development of a topic can often be mapped chronologically. The identification of these texts enables a more accurate search to be undertaken by using *citation indexes* (see Chapter 9). These are indexes that record the number of times a work has been cited (referred to) by other authors. The bibliographical framework for book material is shown in Figure 5.2.

FINDING BOOKS

Most published material is subject to what is called *bibliographical control*. Figure 5.3 gives an overview of the sources that record published materials, including audio-visual and CD ROM.

Time period of publications	Sources recording publications
Distant past	Bibliographies
	Catalogues
	National bibliographies: past editions
	Retrospective listings
	OPACs
Recent past	Electronic bibliographies
	National bibliographies: current editions
	Publishers' catalogues
Present	Trade listings
	Review periodicals and newspapers
Future	Publishers' catalogues
	Current awareness services
	Research registers

Figure 5.1   *The bibliographical time frame for book materials*

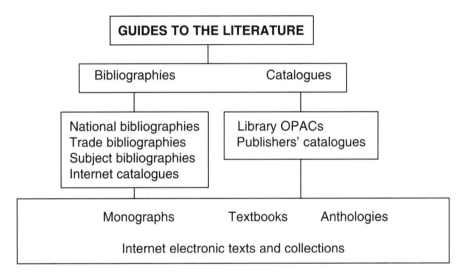

Figure 5.2   *The bibliographical framework for book materials*

When a book or journal is published it is assigned a unique number: for books the number is the International Standard Book Number (ISBN) and for journals it is the International Standard Serial Number (ISSN). Figure 5.4 shows the kind of bibliographical record now included in most books that you can use to construct your citations (see Appendix 4 on citing sources).

It is this bibliographical information that has enabled published and some unpublished materials to be systematically recorded. This enables written work to be recorded in standardized bibliographies. The same system is also used to catalogue books on to OPACs. It is usual therefore to find that a particular book has been allocated the same

Tip: *see Appendix 2 for the Dewey Decimal Classification locations for a selection of subjects and Chapter 1 for an outline of the DDC.*

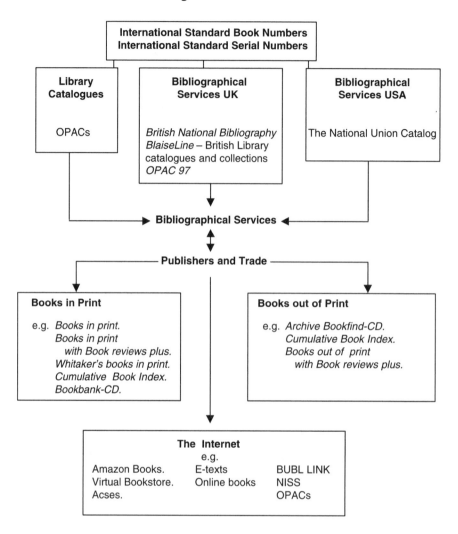

Figure 5.3 *Bibliographical control*

Dewey Decimal number by different libraries that stock the book. Added to this advantage of standardization is the increasing ability to search the bibliographical records on any OPAC in a similar way regardless of the topic.

Identifying useful books

There is no fixed method for assessing the value of a book to your research. To judge the value of a book, first match its topic against your search criteria and search vocabulary by looking at the following:

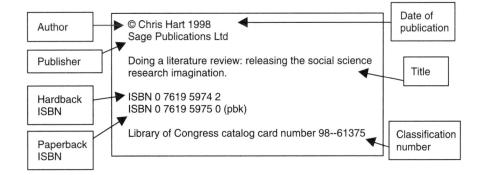

Figure 5.4 *Bibliographical record for a book*

1 **Preface** – look to see if it is really on your topic and appropriate to your level of need.
2 **Biographical notes** – is the author a key contributor to your topic? If he/she is then you probably need to read the book.
3 **Title and subtitle** – do they look relevant? Remember that some books are published under different titles so try and avoid reading the same book twice.
4 **Contents lists** – are any of the contents on your topic?
5 **Publisher** – is the publisher known for publishing books on your topic?
6 **Bibliography** – do the items in the bibliography look familiar or related to your topic?

If a book you think might be relevant is not in your library and all you have is a citation from the catalogue, then do a *citation search* or search for reviews of the book (see Chapter 9 for further details) to help you decide whether it is worth ordering from inter-library loans.

OPACs

There are a number of places you can start from when compiling a list of books on a topic or a methodology. One of the most obvious things to do is to look at what is around you: at the bibliographies in books and articles your library already has. Search for references that look as though they might be useful. The next step is to use local libraries. If you have access to an academic library then that library's collections can be searched. Most academic libraries, electronic catalogues (OPACs) are very easy to use.

OPACs can be searched in various ways. You can search by subject, author, title and key words. For example, if you were searching for 'surveillance' then a key word search would provide 'hits' of books on 'surveillance' and the class mark (DDC) at which they can be found in that library. However, the OPAC would only throw up references to

> **Tip:** *remember that many OPACs can give you access to gateways (e.g. NISS) and numerous online catalogues and indexing and abstracting databases.*

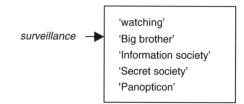

Figure 5.5 *Search vocabulary for 'surveillance'*

books that had the word surveillance in the title. Many items might have relevant material on surveillance but not have the word in the title. This is why it is important to have a good search vocabulary – a list of words and phrases used to search the OPACs and bibliographies. Use subject dictionaries, encyclopaedias and thesauri to determine a useful search vocabulary, remembering to focus, if possible, on nouns. Figure 5.5 shows a search vocabulary for 'surveillance'.

If you have access to the Internet (your public library can provide access) then the OPACs of many other libraries can also be searched. This will provide further references, which can be obtained through inter-library loan. *BUBL Link* provides access to the OPACs of most libraries worldwide. The following gives an indication of the many OPACs now available via *BUBL*:

BUBL Link online public access catalogues 🕸
(address – http://link.bubl.ac.uk/libraryopacs/).

- *National library OPACs in the UK*
  e.g. COPAC: University Research Library Catalogue; Blaise Web; British Library OPAC 97; National History Museum;
- *Subject-specific and research library OPACs in the UK*
  e.g. National Art Library OPAC; Wellcome Institute for the History of Medicine OPAC; Working Class Movement Library OPAC;
- *University OPACs in England, Scotland and Wales*
  e.g. University of Wales Bangor OPAC; University of Wales Cardiff OPAC; Glasgow University OPAC; Edinburgh University OPAC; Warwick University OPAC; Liverpool University OPAC; Oxford University OPAC;
- *College OPACs in England*
  e.g. Selly Oak Colleges; Nene University College Northampton;
- *London University OPACs*
  British Library of Political and Economic Science OPAC; University College London OPAC; Imperial College OPAC: Goldsmith's College OPAC;
- *University OPACs in Ireland*
  e.g. National University of Ireland, Dublin; University of Limerick OPAC; Queen's University Belfast OPAC; St Mary's College Belfast OPAC;

- *Worldwide OPACs*
  e.g. European Commission Library Catalogue; National Library Catalogues; LOCIS: Library of Congress Information System;
- *WebCATS: Library OPACs on the World Wide Web*
  Access to many library catalogues worldwide available via the Internet.

BIBLIOGRAPHICAL SERVICES

Bibliographies need to be consulted to identify items that are not easily accessible through the library OPAC. Bibliographies are more than simple listings of books, they are serious tools for recording what is in print (*current bibliography*) and what has been printed (*retrospective bibliography*). Used in combination the different bibliographical services can be very useful as 'finding tools'. Subject- and author-specific entries allow the researcher to search both a topic and the output of a particular author. The main types of bibliography are: national bibliographies, trade listings, catalogues of national libraries, published bibliographies and catalogues of special libraries, subject bibliographies and guides to bibliographies (bibliographies of bibliographies).

National bibliographies

Many countries have bibliographies that list books which their libraries hold. The two national bibliographies that dominate the English speaking world are:

- **The British National Bibliography (BNB)**
  British Library National Bibliographical Service. This is a weekly classified list, with author/title and subject indexes which accumulate monthly. The list is further cumulated annually. *BNB* lists all materials received by the Legal Deposit Office. Its objective is to be the most comprehensive list of works published in the United Kingdom. *BNB* uses Dewey Decimal Classification to classify entries. *BNB* is also available on CD ROM and online via *Blaise*. The CD ROMs are produced by Chadwyck-Healey and have been issued on a quarterly basis since 1986. CD ROMs are also available for the periods 1950–76 and 1977–85. CD ROM makes searching this invaluable bibliography an efficient and effective use of time. ▣ ☉ ⛫
- **The National Union Catalog: USA books**
  This is the American version of *BNB*. It is based on the Library of Congress Catalog and covers approximately 20 million books. It is available in the UK in many academic libraries in microfiche format and via the British Library's *Portico* gateway. ☉ ⛫

Trade bibliographies

Lists of books 'in print' and 'out of print' are provided by many companies that work in close co-operation with publishers. They provide information on which books are probably still available from publishers. The main trade listing is:

- **Whitaker's books in print**.
  Whitaker (*WBIP*). This lists books available for purchase regardless of when they were published. Retitled in 1978 from *British books in print*, it now lists about half a million titles. A microfiche is also available that shows *Books 1976–1990* that are now out of print. The CD ROM versions of these two are known as **Bookbank** and **Bookbank Op**. The American equivalent of *WBIP* is **Books in Print**, Bowker-Saur. This is arranged according to author, title, subject and publisher. **Books in print with book review plus** is an enhanced service that provides book reviews. ⊙ 🕸 ☎

Other listings include the following:

- **The Bookseller**.
  Whitaker's. This is a guide to books published each week. Two editions (one in the spring, the other in the autumn) list books to be published within the next six months. Contents are arranged according to broad subject categories. 📖
- **Global bookbank**.
  Whitaker and Bowker-Saur. This brings together data on about two million books currently available in English from around the world. ⊙ 🕸 ☎
- **Cumulative book index**.
  H.W. Wilson. This lists books in English from around the world. Published since 1898. It is also available online through Wilsonline and on CD ROM. ⊙ 🕸 ☎
- **Bookwise-CD**.
  Published by Book Data Ltd. A database of over 900,000 titles available in the UK, including forthcoming books. ⊙

There are other listings, some of which provide details of books out of print, such as, *Archive book find-CD*, *Book find-Online*, *Book bank-CD* and *Books out of print*.

Publishers' catalogues

Most publishers produce catalogues, and these can be useful guides to recent and forthcoming publications. Key publishers of academic books include, Sage, Blackwell, Oxford University Press and Routledge. Most publishers now have web sites where their catalogues can be searched. There are also many booksellers on the web along with other web-based services that will search publishers' catalogues.

- **Amazon books**.
  (address – www.amazon.com/).
  The 2.5 million records in the database can be searched by author, title, subject, ISBN or key word. 🕸
- **Virtual bookstore**.
  (address – www.national-publishing.co.uk/).
  The entire Stationery Office (UK) catalogue with approximately 10,000 new publications each year. 🕸
- **ACSES**.
  (address – www.acses.com/).
  Substantial database of books and other materials arranged by general subject. 🕸
- **WebCATS**.
  (address – www.lights.com/webcats/).
  An Internet gateway to a range of web-based catalogues including those of publishers. 🕸

Subject bibliographies

Bibliographies on particular disciplines such as sociology, English and education are regularly produced by specific organizations, though not all are published. An example of a subject bibliography is *Resources for nursing research: an annotated bibliography*, by Clamp, C.G.L., Ballard, M.P. and Gough, S. (London: Library Association, 1994). Consult directories of organizations and directories of special libraries to see if there are any libraries or collections that might be of use in your work. The most comprehensive subject bibliography in the social sciences is the:

- **International bibliography of the social sciences**.
  British Library of Political and Economic Science: London School of Economics. This is one of the most important and valuable bibliographies for social science scholars. It covers all the disciplines in the social sciences along with the humanities and some arts. Annual supplements were published up until 1989. Since then the LSE has compiled the annual **National bibliography of sociology** that is published by Routledge. This is updated by monthly issues of the **International current awareness service: sociology and related disciplines**, which lists books, articles and some research reports. 🕸 📖

Other major bibliographic databases include:

- **MLA international bibliography**.
  Modern Language Association of America. From 1963 a humanities-based database of monographs, articles and other scholarly works. Silver Platter CD ROM version has links to full text sources. 📖 ☉ 🏛
- **OCLC education library**.
  International bibliography of educational materials spanning 400 years (sub-set of *WorldCat*, the OCLC Online Union Catalog). ☉ 🏛

Published bibliographies and catalogues of specialist libraries

Many libraries from around the world produce and sometimes publish bibliographies of special collections. You should find out if a special library exists that might have material on your topic that is not available elsewhere. Details of libraries in the United Kingdom can be found in a number of directories, such as *British archives* by Janet Foster and Julia Sheppard (London: Macmillan, 1999) and *Directory of special collections in Western Europe* by Alison Gallico (1993). Most notable people, ideas, movements and theories, and even places, have been studied at some time and these studies will have resulted in a bibliography. Some of the bibliographies are academic pieces of work while others are incomplete catalogues of ad hoc collections. The following examples are just a few of the many thousands of bibliographies available:

> **Tip:** *look for archives on the Internet relevant to your topic. Many have extensive bibliographies.*

- **The library of John Locke**.
  Harrison, J. and Laslett, P. Oxford: Oxford University Press, 1965. Compiled by academics of the Oxford Bibliographical Society, this monographical bibliography lists the contents of Locke's own library. This work gives an essential understanding of the intellectual context in which Locke worked. Bibliographies like this are usually accompanied by introductory essays giving details of the person, the time in which they lived and their work (published and unpublished). This bibliography contains an essay on the book acquisition habits of Locke. 📖
- **Feminist archives**.
  There are a number of collections partially catalogued in the UK. One is at Trinity Road Library, Bristol BS2 ONW and another at the Department of Applied Social Studies, Bradford University. Both have collections of books and other materials dating from the 1960s. 📖
- **Education**.
  Two notable collections on education in the UK are in the Museum of the History of Education, at the University of Leeds and the Institute of Education Library at the University of London. Both have extensive collections of books relating to and used in British education from the turn of the twentieth century. 📖

- **ArchivesUSA**.
  Chadwyck-Healey database of primary source materials from over 4,500 US manuscript depositories with a directory of depositories, subject indexing of 42,000 collections and records from the National Union Catalog of Manuscript Collections compiled by the Library of Congress. ⊙ 🕸

INTERNET RESOURCES

There are many sources on the Internet where subject bibliographies can be consulted. The following are some current web resources for archives, methodology and electronic books and texts.

> **Tip:** *a simple card index can be an effective and efficient method for keeping track of Internet sources.*

Internet archives

- **The Marx/Engels archive**.
  (address – http://csf.colorado.edu/psn/marx/).
  Extensive archive on Marx and Engels with substantial bibliographies.
- **NOEMA: The collaborative bibliography of women in philosophy**.
  (address – http://billyboy.ius.indiana.edu/womeninphilosophy.html).
  Biographies and bibliographies for over 5,000 women in subjects such as aesthetics, art, epistemology, logic, metaphysics, science and other academic subjects. 🕸
- **The Wellek library lecturer bibliographies**.
  (address – http://sun3.lib.uci.edu/indiv/scctr/Wellek/index.html).
  A site sponsored by the University of California, Irvine, based on the annual Wellek lecturers, including Jacques Derrida, Jean-François Lyotard and Edward Said. Bibliographies are provided, along with interviews. 🕸
- **Ludwig Wittgenstein**.
  (address – www.ags.uci.edu/~bcarver/ludwig.html).
  A comprehensive Internet-based archive and resource with bibliographies and links to online texts. 🕸
- **BUBL: Bibliographies** and **Book and text collections**.
  (address – http://bubl.ac.uk/link/bibliographies.html).
  (address – http://bubl.ac.uk/link/types/books.html).
  A growing list of bibliographies (65+) on a wide range of subjects and text collections worldwide including access to the complete works of Shakespeare, Lewis Carroll and Dickens. 🕸
- **Digital librarian: women's resources**.
  (address – www.servtech.com/).
  A–Z listing of resources on women's issues including bibliographical resources. 🕸

- **SocioSite: feminism and women's issues**.
  (address – www.pscw.uva.nl/sociosite/).
  A well organized set of resources including bibliographical resources on feminism and women's issues. ✹

<table>
<tr><td>

Tip: *for more information on electronic texts see Chapter 8 on archives.*

</td><td>

There is a rapidly growing list of commercial Internet-based resources with bibliographies and primary source materials. *Rare Books Online* (Gale Publications) has some very interesting collections including *Witchcraft in Europe*

</td></tr>
</table>

and America (address – www.witchcraft.psmedia.com/) that includes many classic texts, writings, Church documents, trial transcripts and bibliographic citations.

Internet sources on methodology and data collection techniques

Other useful web sites are those associated with professional associations, research centres and individuals. Here are some related to research methodology which have bibliographic resources.

- **Bill Trochim's Centre for social research methods**.
  (address – http://trochim.human.cornell.edu/index.html).
  Very good resource for social sciences includes an online research methods textook. ✹
- **Institute for historic research bibliographies**.
  (address – http://www.ihr.sas.ac.uk/cwis/aahcbib.html). ✹
- **The Qualitative Report (QR)**.
  (address – www.nova.edu/ssss/QR/index.html).
  Online journal dedicated to qualitative inquiry. ✹
- **Research resources for the social sciences**.
  (address – www.socsciresearch.com/).
  An online textbook of resources, including bibliographies, for the social scientist, based on Craig McKie's *Using the Web for social research*, New York: McGraw-Hill Ryerson 1997. ✹
- **Research methodology and statistics**.
  (address – www.pscw.uva.nl/sociosite/).
  List of links with descriptions from SocioSite categorized into methodology, survey methods, qualitative research, statistics, software and journals. Also see SocioSite's category on theories and perspectives. ✹

Internet electronic books and texts

A number of meta sites provide listings and links to electronic books and texts. Here are some useful gateways:

- **WebGEMS: E-text**.
  (address – www.fpsol.com/gems/).
  Select list of electronic text resources including the Avalon Project and Project Gutenberg. 🕸
- **HUMBUL: Electronic texts**.
  (address – http://info.ox.ac.uk/oucs/humanities/international/).
  From the HUMBUL multi-subject gateway a quality list of links to electronic text resources including **Athena** (vast collection of e-texts), **Books online** (directory) and **Oxford text archives**. 🕸
- **Online texts collection**.
  (address – www.ipl.org/). **The Internet Public Library**'s links categorized by Dewey into subject areas and an A–Z provides a comprehensive set of lists of e-texts, resources and major directories. 🕸
- **Galileo: electronic texts**.
  (address – www.usg.edu/galileo/).
  This multi-subject gateway is a well organized set of resources with links to many subject areas and chosen directories such as the online books page (links to 10,000 English language e-texts). 🕸
- **Digital Librarian: electronic texts and primary resources**.
  (address – www.servtech.com/).
  Comprehensive listing of multi-language e-texts and digitized primary sources including e-texts directories. 🕸

FINDING BIBLIOGRAPHIES

There are guides to national bibliographies and subject bibliographies. The most relevant general guides to national bibliographies are:

- **Bibliographic services throughout the world**.
  UNESCO. This is a multi-volume set with each set covering a period of five years. 🕸 📖
- **An annotated guide to current national bibliographies**.
  Bell, B. and Alexandria, L. Chadwyck-Healey, 1986. 📖
- **Guide to current national bibliographies in the third world**.
  2nd edn. Gorman, G.E. and Mills, J.J. London: Hans Zell, 1987. This covers large regions (e.g the Caribbean) rather than individual countries. 📖
- **Bibliographic index: a cumulative bibliography of bibliographies**.
  Wilson, 1939 to date. ▤ ⊙

Subject-specific guides to bibliographies include the following:

- **Walford's guide to reference material: social and historical sciences, philosophy and religion**.
  7th edn, Vol. 2. Day, A. and Walsh, M. (eds). London: Library Association Publishing, 1997. 📖 🕸
- **Walford's guide to reference material: generalia, language & literature, the arts**.
  Vol. 3. Chalcraft, A., Prytherch, R. and Willis, S. (eds). London: Library Association Publishing, 1998. 📖 🕸
- **Sources of information in the social sciences**.
  3rd edn. Webb, W.H., Beals, A.R. and White, C.M. Chicago: American Library Association, 1986. 📖
- **The humanities: a selective guide to information sources**. Blazek, R. and Aversa, E. Englewood Cliffs, NJ: Libraries Unlimited, 1988. 📖

Some libraries might have a rare book collection on a subject. To find out if such a collection exists consult the following type of directory.

- **A directory of rare book and special collections in the United Kingdom and the Republic of Ireland**. 2nd edn. Bloomfield, B.C. and Potts, K. (eds). London: Library Association, 1997. 📖

If no relevant special library or collection is listed this does not mean one does not exist. Many private collections that are not listed are often known about by librarians in special libraries. So if a library exists that has *some* connections with your subject, ask its librarian about what other similar collections exist and you may discover a more relevant collection.

THE BRITISH LIBRARY

The British Library has one of the largest collections of printed materials in the world, with materials dating from before the 1500s. The main bibliographical service is the *British National Bibliography* (*BNB*), a national record of publishing in the British Isles since 1950, available in print, CD ROM and online. Through its National Bibliographic Services (NBS), the British Library now has over 17 million bibliographical records in 22 databases. Approximately 90 per cent of material published before 1800 is not found in the American equivalent, the *National Union Catalog*. There are many services provided by the British Library, some of which are shown in Figure 5.6 and described below.

BNB on CD-ROM

The *British National Bibliography* on CD-ROM, the national record of publishing in the United Kingdom and Ireland since 1950. Flexible and efficient searching is possible of 25 indexes to help identify relevant

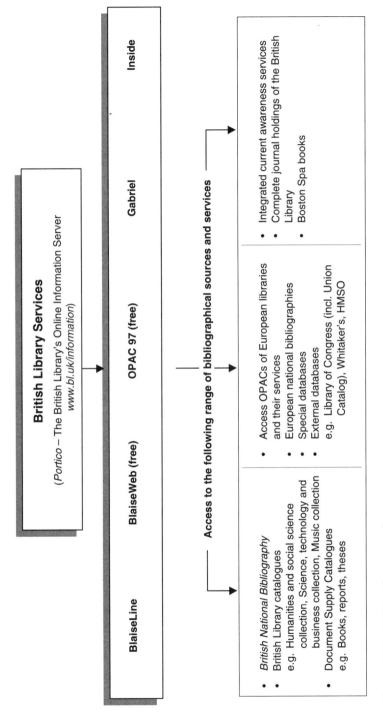

British Library Services

(*Portico* – The British Library's Online Information Server
www.bl.uk/information)

| BlaiseLine | BlaiseWeb (free) | OPAC 97 (free) | Gabriel | Inside |

Access to the following range of bibliographical sources and services

- *British National Bibliography*
- British Library catalogues
  e.g. Humanities and social science collection, Science, technology and business collection, Music collection
- Document Supply Catalogues
  e.g. Books, reports, theses

- Access OPACs of European libraries and their services
- European national bibliographies
- Special databases
- External databases
  e.g. Library of Congress (incl. Union Catalog), Whitaker's, HMSO

- Integrated current awareness services
- Complete journal holdings of the British Library
- Boston Spa books

Figure 5.6 *British Library services*

material quickly and easily by author, title, key words, ISBN, publication details, subject headings (including Library of Congress), series, Dewey class number and many more. Current awareness is available and with over 6,000 records of new and forthcoming titles added every month, items added since the last cumulation can be identified with a New Records search. All *BNB* since 1986 is on a single CD ROM.

OPAC 97

OPAC 97 is a free service that will allow you to find out what material is held in the major reference and document supply collections of the British Library. In many cases it will also be possible to request copies of document supply material from the Library's Document Supply Centre (BLDSC) at Boston Spa. Good 'General help' and 'Help with searching' are available for those who are new to OPAC 97. For a wider range of databases and many additional facilities the British Library offers *Blaise*, a fee-based online bibliographical information service, and *Inside*, offering article title records from 20,000 journals and 70,000 conferences. Other OPACs that may be of interest can be accessed through *NISS* (National Information Services and Systems) and the Library of Congress.

Reference collections represented on OPAC 97 include:

1 **Humanities and Social Sciences collection (1975—)**. Items found in this collection are generally held in the main reading room in London. The coverage includes humanities and social sciences information, popular science and psychology holdings and resources relating to Africa.
2 **Science, Technology and Business collection (1975—)**. The collection includes scientific, technological and business information in many forms.
3 **Music collection (1980—)**. Items found in this collection are generally held in the Music Library reading room which is based within Official Publications and Social Sciences (OP&SS) in London. This is one of the world's finest collections of printed music.

Document supply collections represented on OPAC 97 include **Books and reports collection (1980—)**. This covers millions of British and overseas books, reports and UK theses. Items found in this collection are held in stock at the Document Supply Centre at Boston Spa. Users can normally consult material in the BLDSC reading room or order a photocopy from the BLDSC.

Blaise

Blaise, the British Library's online information service, offers access to over 17 million bibliographical records for materials collected worldwide by the Library on a variety of subjects since 1980. *BlaiseWeb* offers simple access to

Blaise, while a more detailed service is offered under the existing *BlaiseLine* fee-based service. Services provided include *British National Bibliography*, British Library catalogues which include Document Supply Centre catalogues, and external databases including Library of Congress, Whitaker's and HMSO.

Boston Spa Books

The CD ROM database records over 800,000 books collected by the British Library Document Supply Centre since 1980. This database provides details of mainly English language monographs from all over the world which present a serious scholarly approach to a subject; it also includes information on theses, official publications and reports and translations. Over 50,000 monographs, theses, official publications and reports are added to the database each year. It can be used for title searching, reference verification and checking inter-library loan availability prior to placing requests. All books found on this database are available on loan from the British Library Document Supply Centre. Other CD ROM databases include: Boston Spa Conferences, Boston Spa Serials, and Inside Conferences.

BNBMARC

Weekly file containing records of new and forthcoming publications in the UK and Ireland.

LCMARC

Weekly file of records for monographs catalogued by the Library of Congress and covering US imprints and publications worldwide in English and many other languages.

Gabriel

The World Wide Web server for Europe's national libraries, this acts as a bridge by providing a single point of access for the retrieval of information about their functions, services and collections. Information about individual national libraries is provided, including details of their history, policy, important collections and services. Links are offered to pages in which online services of the chosen library are described, e.g. WWW and gopher services, OPACs, national union catalogues, national bibliographies, and special databases.

Inside

A fully integrated current awareness and document ordering service, via the Web or on CD-ROM, that allows you to search, order and receive documents held at the British Library. Allows a search of 20,000 of the world's most valued research journals and over 70,000 conference proceedings at paper-title level. The database expands by over two million articles every year and can also be used to search the complete journal holdings of the British Library Document Supply Centre to check on availability of 250,000 journal titles, covering over 300 years.

SUMMARY OF THIS CHAPTER

- There are a number of bibliographical databases and services that can be used to find books on your topic and on methodology.
- The main sources are your library's OPAC, Walford and *BNB*.
- Many special libraries and special collections have catalogues that can usually be searched.
- A subject librarian will often have knowledge of bibliographies and special collections, so consult them about your search.
- Electronic texts are a good source for bibliographies and for primary source materials.

6

Finding journal articles

This chapter will show you:

- how to find indexes and abstracts relevant to your topic
- how to find articles on your topic
- how to find print and electronic journals

Journals (also known as periodicals) are one of the most important sources of information about research, debate and issues on a topic. Many journals are now available in electronic formats (e.g. CD ROM, online and via the Internet). The popularity of journals resides in their subject- and topic-specific content and regularity of publication. They are usually not subject to the publication delays common to books. The main categories of journal relevant to research are *learned journals* and *professional journals*.

- Learned journals report on developments in scholarly research in the form of articles which are normally refereed by peers in the field of expertise to which the journal is dedicated.
- Professional journals are newsletter-type publications of associations and are written for members of the association. They often contain a mixture of news, brief articles and letters along with information on forthcoming events such as conferences.

Increasingly abstracting and indexing services for journals are available on CD ROM and online as *full-text*. This means that the CD ROM or web site provides access to the full-text of articles which have been indexed by the service. Therefore there is no need to search the CD ROM and then locate a copy of the relevant journal. Like book material, journal material (by which is meant articles and book reviews), indexes and abstracts are subject to a general bibliographical framework (see Figure 6.1).

FINDING ARTICLES

The main type of tool that will help you to find articles on your topic is that of indexes and abstracts. These are reference sources which record in an

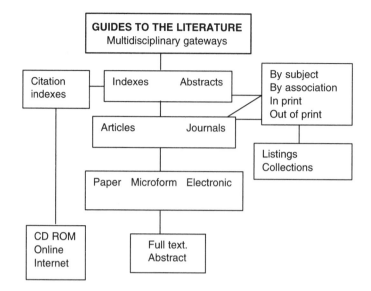

Figure 6.1   *The bibliographical framework for articles and journals*

organized way the contents of journals. The majority of articles published in journals are indexed and many are subject to abstracting services. Most abstract and indexing services are now available in several formats including print, online and CD ROM. Searching electronic databases is described in Chapters 10 and 11.

> **Tip:** *remember that if an article is not in your library the librarian should be able to order a copy for you.*

Using knowledge of the bibliographical framework relevant to articles will give you a means to define the time frame for your search. If you need to do a state-of-the-art search then you will be aiming to find articles published within the last six months – so many may not yet have been indexed. You will therefore need to use *alerting* or *current awareness services*. Some of these are identified later in this chapter. An alerting service lets you know what has just been published or is about to be published. Alerting services attempt to bridge the gap between the time an article is published in a journal and the time when it is indexed in an indexing journal. The time frame of indexing and abstracting services is shown in Figure 6.2.

Indexing and abstracting services

A number of organizations produce subject-based indexes of published articles. In some cases the indexes are supplemented with abstracts, which are summaries of the content of an article with some bibliographical information. The different types of abstract are summarized in Figure 6.3. Abstracts allow

> **Tip:** *see Appendix 7 for a list of indexes and abstracts for a selection of disciplines.*

.

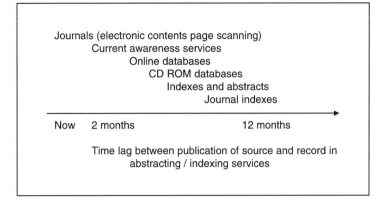
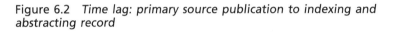

Journals (electronic contents page scanning)
Current awareness services
Online databases
CD ROM databases
Indexes and abstracts
Journal indexes

Now   2 months   12 months

Time lag between publication of source and record in
abstracting / indexing services

Figure 6.2   *Time lag: primary source publication to indexing and abstracting record*

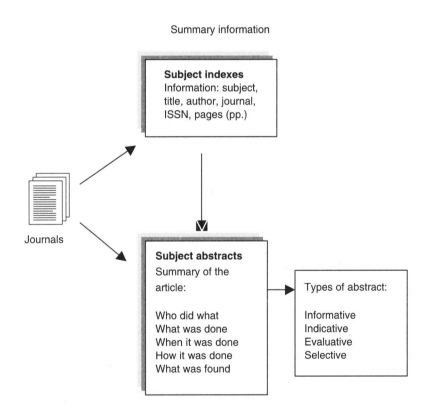

Summary information

Subject indexes
Information: subject,
title, author, journal,
ISSN, pages (pp.)

Journals

Subject abstracts
Summary of the
article:

Who did what
What was done
When it was done
How it was done
What was found

Types of abstract:

Informative
Indicative
Evaluative
Selective

Figure 6.3   *Indexes and abstracts*

you to assess the relevance of a document before obtaining it. In some cases the abstract may be sufficient in itself, as a substitute when the document is unavailable. When you cite an abstract the term *ghost entry* is used to refer to documents known about but not seen.

The journals of most subject disciplines are covered by one or more indexing and abstracting service. Some of the main (multi-subject) indexing and abstracting services for the social sciences, arts and humanities are shown below. When

> **Tip:** *advice on abstracts and their use is given in Chapter 3.*

beginning any search always consult these even when a specific index or abstracting service is available. The general rule of thumb is, search the general (multi-subject indexes and abstracts) and then the specific (subject indexes and abstracts).

Multi-subject indexes and abstracts

The following are some of the major indexing and abstracting services. When combined, these cover nearly all quality publications in the social sciences, arts and humanities.

- **Applied social science index and abstracts (ASSIA)**.
  Bowker-Saur. Bi-monthly covering 500 journals. Available as ASSIA Plus that contains a backfile to 1987 and as ASSIAnet.co.uk, a web current awareness version of ASSIA. ⊙ 🕸 ☎
- **British humanities index**.
  Bowker-Saur. A quarterly publication that indexes all the major journals in economics, politics, law, education, ecology and drama. Available as BHI Plus 1985 to the present, as BHInet.co.uk, a web current awareness version of BHI with records back to 1984, and as BHI Archive *Plus* incorporating all the records from 1962 (when BHI was first published) to 1984 with those on BHI Plus to 1997. ⊙ 🕸 📖 ☎
- **Wilson humanities abstracts**.
  Abstracting and indexing of 400 English language periodicals covering archaeology, classical studies, communication, art, philosophy, history, music, linguistics, literature and religion. The full-text version is Wilson humanities index full-text and is available online from SilverPlatter. ⊙ ☎
- **Wilson social science abstracts**.
  Abstracting and indexing of 513 English language periodicals covering anthropology, criminology, economics, law, medicine, planning, politics, psychology, public administration, social sciences, social work, sociology and women's studies. The full-text version is Wilson social science abstracts full-text and is available online from SilverPlatter. ⊙ ☎
- **International bibliography of the social sciences extra**.
  CD ROM version from SilverPlatter with over 2,600 social science journals indexed. ⊙

- **UnCover**.
  (address – http://uncweb.carl.org/).

Indexing service for over 18,000 journal titles across many subjects with over eight million article citations. A powerful service.

Subject indexes and abstracts

There are numerous indexes and abstracts for the different disciplines and subjects of the social sciences, humanities and arts. Here are some of the most popular services, relevant to many subjects:

- **Psychology abstracts**.
  American Psychological Society. Abstract and indexing of most psychology and related journals and some book chapters from edited collections. Also available in the following variations, PsycINFO, Psychlit and ClinPSYC, which have differences in coverage and availability. Through its SilverPlatter version it has links to the Internet and some full-text sources. ⊙ ✿ ☎
- **Sociological abstracts**.
  Produced for the American and International Sociological Associations by Cambridge Scientific Abstracts. This is similar to Psychology abstracts. It has very wide coverage and dates back to 1963. Also available as Sociofile. Through its SilverPlatter version it has links to the Internet and some full-text sources. ⊙ ✿ ☎
- **Current index to journals in education**.
  Educational Resources Information Centre – US Department of Education. A monthly guide to current periodical literature in education indexing over 775 major journal titles going back to 1966. Also available as ERIC. Through its SilverPlatter version it has links to the Internet and some full-text sources. ⊙ ✿ ☎

Finding indexing and abstracting services

To find relevant indexing and abstracting services consult guides to the literature and specialist directories. The guides to the literature (see Chapter 2) will provide information on long-established services. In addition to the following sources, however, subject librarians should be able to provide information on the latest electronic indexes and abstracts.

Guides to current index and abstracts:

- **The index and abstracts directory**.
  Ebsco Publishing. Regular updates. 📖
- **Walford's guide to reference material**.
  Vol. 2. *Social and historical sciences, philosophy and religion*. Day, A. and Walsh, M. (eds). 7th edn. London: LA Publishing, 1997. 📖 ✿

- **Walford's guide to reference material**.
  Vol. 3. *Generalia, language and literature, the arts*. Chalcraft, A., Prytherch, R. and Willis, S. (eds). 7th edn. London: LA Publishing, 1998. 📖 ⍟
- **Printed reference materials and related sources of information**.
  Lea, P.W. 3rd edn. London: Library Association, 1990. 📖
- **SilverPlatter database guide**.
  (address – www.silverplatter.com/).
  Covers a very wide range of subjects and disciplines with links via the Internet (SilverLinker Database) to the specific abstracts and indexes. ⊙ ☎ ⍟
- **Gale directory of databases**.
  Comprehensive guide to over 14,000 databases publicly available. Available from SilverPlatter and from Gale as *Gale Directory of databases online*. ⊙ ☎

A number of publications attempt to provide indexes of *older journal materials*. Guides to the literature, and subject librarians, should be able to help identify if a retrospective index exists. Some examples of these publications are:

- **The Essex reference index: British journals on politics and sociology**.
  MacDonald, K.I. London: Macmillan, 1975. 📖
- **Retrospective film index to film periodicals**.
  Batty, L. New York: Bowker-Saur, 1975. 📖
- **Wellesley index to Victorian periodicals 1824–1900**.
  London: Routledge, 1999. ⊙

Also look out for the increasing digitization of early journal collections such as *The Internet library of early journals* from the Universities of Birmingham, Leeds, Manchester and Oxford (address – www.bodley.ox.-ac.uk/ilej/start.htm).

Citation indexes

A special form of index is the citation index. This is based on the simple concept that references (citations) in a book or article will indicate subject relationships between the current article and previous publications. Most citation indexes are published by the Institute for Scientific Information in Philadelphia and are available on subscription. Many indexes of journal contents are now combined with citation indexes of works cited by those articles indexed. Citation-based indexes such as Social Sci Search are available online from Datastar and Dialog (these are described in Chapter 11) and UnCover, from Blackwell (described below). The traditional citation indexes are to be

> **Tip:** *advice on how to use citation indexes can be found in Chapter 9.*

found on the ISI Web of science (address – www.isinet.com/) and are normally available only through an academic library. The main citation indexes relevant to the social sciences, arts and humanities are:

Social sciences citation index   ISI. This is produced three times a year and covers over 1,400 multidisciplinary journals. The index consists of three main parts:

1   *Citation index*: shows which previously published item is being referred to in the current literature, who is citing it and in what journals. This can be used to identify a key book or article published in the past. Looking up the author will tell you which other researchers have also cited that work recently. This is given as a number that corresponds to bibliographical entries in the source index. Having noted all the current citations to the key article, the searcher can turn to the source index.
2   *Source index*: this provides full bibliographical details on the citations.
3   *Permutem index*: this is a permuted title word index to article titles. It pairs all significant words in a title, e.g. mothers, surrogates, thus producing a 'natural language' indexing system. The pairs are listed alphabetically and are linked to the names of authors who use them. Authors can therefore be found through keyword searching. There is also an index of corporate addresses. This can be used to find out what has been published by a corporate body, such as a research centre.

Arts and humanities citation index   ISI. Very similar to the above. This covers over 1,100 international arts and humanities journals. About 100,000 records are added annually and the 1980–89 cumulation holds over million records. Not only are subjects from over 25 disciplines covered but also included are book reviews, theatre reviews, bibliographies, editorials, film reviews, art exhibition reviews and poetry.

FINDING JOURNALS

There are several thousand journals regularly published around the world. Most of these are published by commercial publishers in association with universities or groups of academics who act as editorial boards. Lists of journals in a particular subject area can be constructed by consulting guides, abstracts and indexes. Abstracting and indexing services usually provide lists of journals covered by the service. These lists show the range of journals publishing material on a subject. Guides, however, are the more traditional means of locating relevant journal titles. The following are some useful guides to most journal titles, including newspapers.

Finding lists of journals

- **Willings press guide**.
  East Grinstead: British Media Publications, 1871—. 📖
- **Current British journals**.
  Published by the British Library Document Supply Centre. Available on CD ROM as **Boston Spa serials**. It contains over 350,000 records. ⊙ 📖 ☎
- **The standard periodicals directory 1999**.
  New York: Oxbridge Communications, regular updates. Guide to United States and Canadian periodicals. 📖
- **Ulrich's international periodicals directory**.
  (address – www.ulrichsweb.com/). Bowker-Saur, regularly updated. CD ROM and online versions have links to indexes, document ordering services and evaluations. ⊙ 📖 ☎
- **Journal listings**.
  (address – http://bubl.ac.uk/link/types/journallists.html). Listing of journals for 90+ subjects and topics. 🕸

Finding periodicals no longer in print

This can be done by consulting the following type of general and specific retrospective bibliographies:

- **British union catalogue of periodicals**.
  London: Butterworths. Ceased publication in 1980 and was superseded by **Serials in the British Library**. 📖 ⊙
- **New Cambridge bibliography of English literature**.
  5 vols. Cambridge: Cambridge University Press, 1969–77. 📖
- **The Waterloo directory of Victorian periodicals, 1824–1900**.
  Wolff, M. Oxford: Pergamon Press, 1980. 📖
- **World list of scientific periodicals published in the years 1900–1960**.
  4th edn. London: Butterworths, 1963–65. 📖
- **Women's magazines, 1693–1968**.
  London: Michael Joseph, 1970. 📖
- **Serial publications in the British parliamentary papers, 1900–1968: a bibliography**.
  Chicago: American Library Association, 1971. 📖
- **Feminist periodicals, 1855–1984: an annotated critical bibliography of British, Irish, Commonwealth and international titles**.
  Doughan, D. and Sanchez, D. Brighton: Harvester Press, 1987. 📖
- **Cumulative index of sociology journals, 1971–1985**.
  Lantz, J.C. Washington, DC: American Sociological Association, 1987. 📖

Finding out what library holds which journals

To find out what library holds a particular journal a range of services exists such as UnCover (address – http://uncweb.carl.org/) and publications such as the following:

- **University of London list of serials**.
  London: The University Library, 1979—. 📖
- **Union list of American studies periodicals in UK libraries**.
  Boston Spa: BLDSC and Standing Conference of National and University Libraries, 1983. 📖

Finding electronic journals and journal collections

A growing number of Internet sources provide access to collections of electronic journals on a range of subjects. The following sites tend to act as gateways to e-journal collections, contents listings and (though often you have to pay a subscription) to full-text sources. The combination of Edina and Ingenta provides a comprehensive coverage of key journals in the social sciences, arts and humanities.

Gateways to electronic journals
- **BUBL: Journal collections**.
  (address – http://bubl.ac.uk/link/types/journals.html).
  Listings of journals for a wide range of subjects. Includes links to **EDINA periodical contents index** and **Ingenta journals**. 🕸
- **EDINA periodicals contents index**.
  (address – http://edina.ed.ac.uk/pci/).
  Detailed online access to the contents pages of over 2,750 journals in the social sciences and humanities and over 10 million journal articles since the eighteenth century. 🕸 ☎
- **Ingenta journals**.
  (address – www.ingenta.com and www.bids.ac.uk/).
  Provides access to a growing range of full-text journals from key academic journal publishers. Contents pages can be searched for free. 🕸 ☎

The following are generally *meta-directories* (lists and links to many e-journals) available via the Internet and many provide quality links to full-text sources.

Directories of electronic journals
- **ARL directory of electronic journals, newsletters, and academic discussion lists**.
  (address – http://arl.cni.org/scomm/edir/).

The web version of the 7th edition of the *Directory of Electronic Journals, Newsletters and Academic Discussion Lists* contains descriptions and links to 7,000 listings of journals, newsletters, zines, and professional e-conferences accessible via the Internet. Previous editions are available without restriction but the newest edition is restricted to subscribers. 🕸

- **CIC electronic journals collection**.
  (address – http://ejournals.cic.net/).
  Collaborative project among member libraries of CICNET (Universities and colleges in the USA) that provides catalogued access to a managed collection of electronic journals. See also their related project, CICNet E-Serials Archive. 🕸

- **Digital libraries: electronic journal and text archives**.
  (address – www.ifla.org/II/etext.htm).
  This is a guide to many of the major electronic journal and text indexes and/or archives. It is a very useful resource which includes the following: bibliography, electronic journals, electronic texts, electronic media, and electronic text research centres. 🕸

- **The world-wide web virtual library: e-journals**.
  (address – www.edoc.com/ejournal/).
  The Virtual Library on Electronic Journals includes access to hundreds of electronic journals as well as to a number of other e-journal archives. One of the most comprehensive collections and ways to access electronic journals and newsletters. Categories include: academic and reviewed journals, e-mail newsletters, magazines, and newspapers. 🕸

- **Ejournal SiteGuide: a metaSource**.
  (address – www.library.ubc.ca/ejour/).
  Provides a selected and annotated set of links to sites for e-journals, which in turn provide links to individual titles and/or to other collections of links. 🕸

- **Full-text archives of scholarly society serial publications: University of Waterloo Library**.
  (address – www.lib.uwaterloo.ca/society/full-text_soc.html).
  From the Scholarly Societies Project of the University of Waterloo comes a set of links to full-text archives of some serial publications of scholarly societies. Most, but not all, of these publications are newsletters or similar to newsletters; a small number are research publications. Serials representing several dozen learned societies are present. 🕸

- **NewJour: electronic journal and newsletter archive**.
  (address – http://gort.ucsd.edu/newjour/).
  This is the archive for NewJour, the Internet list for new journals and newsletters available on the Internet with a comprehensive searchable archive. 🕸

- **Scholarly journals distributed via the world-wide web: University of Houston**.
  (address – http://info.lib.uh.edu/wj/webjour.html).

This University of Houston Libraries directory provides links to established Web-based scholarly journals and offers access to English language article files without requiring user registration or fees. 🕸

- **Serials in cyberspace: collections, resources and services**.
  (address – www.uvm.edu/~bmaclenn/).
  A large reference site that indexes e-journal collections. Contents: sites with electronic journal collections and services, academic/research sites (USA), academic/research sites (outside of the USA), and miscellaneous collections and resources. 🕸

- **Electronic journals database**.
  (address – http://biblio.kbsi.re.kr/yellow/index.html).
  Indexes and links to nearly 10,000 journal titles. 🕸

Many meta-directories such as the following can keep you up to date on new e-journals.

- **Humanities hub: selected resources for the social sciences and humanities**.
  (address — www.gu.edu.au/cgi-bin/g-code?/gwis/hub/qa/hub.home.html).
  A large and well organized compilation of resources with easy access. 🕸

- **Digital librarian**.
  (address – www.servtech.com/).
  A–Z listing of selections of the best of the web. 🕸

- **SocioSite**.
  (address – www.pscw.uva.nl/sociosite/).
- A long but well organized list of links with descriptions. 🕸
- **Galileo**.
- (address – www.usg.edu/galileo/).
  Selective links to general and specific resources. 🕸

Finding electronic subject journals

A growing number of subjects now have Internet journals dedicated to them. The major multi-subject gateways (e.g. BUBL, Edina, Ingenta, NISS, SOSIG,) normally list some of those that are refereed and therefore have quality control but also consult the following for subject lists:

- **SocioSite**.
  (address – www.pscw.uva.nl/sociosite/). 🕸
- **Internet public library**.
  (address – www.ipl.org/). 🕸

The following is a list of the more well known resources which have links to other e-journals in their topic area.

Anthropology
- **Anthropology index online**.
  (address – http://lucy.ukc.ac/cgi-bin/uncgi/Search_AI/search_bib_ai/anthind/).
  The index to journals in the Museum of Mankind from 1970 to 1993. 🕸

Economics and finance
- **NetEc**.
  (address – http://netec.mcc.ac.uk/NetEc.html).
  The largest and most important economics resource currently on the Internet with subdivisions leading to articles and working papers. 🕸
- **WebEc**.
  http://netec.mcc.ac.uk/%7eadnetec/WecEc/journals.html).
  A listing of economic journals in print. Part of the WWW Virtual Library project. 🕸
- **ECONbase**.
  (address – www.elsevier.nl/inca/homepage/sae/econbase/).
  Publishers' database of 9,000 articles published in economics and finance journals by Elsevier with abstracts and journal contents. 🕸

Psychology
- **Psycholoquy**.
  (address – www.cogsci.soton.ac.uk/psycholoquy/).
  Highly regarded peer-reviewed e-journal sponsored by the American Psychological Association. 🕸
- **Electronic journals in psychology**.
  (address – www.cycor.ca/Psych/jours.html).
  Listing of psychology and related journals in print and electronic. 🕸
- **Psychology journals**.
  (address – www.wiso.uni-augsburg.de/sozio/hartmann/psycho/html).
  A very long list of psychology journals. 🕸

Sociology
- **Electronic journal of sociology**.
  (address – www.sociology.org/).
  Peer-reviewed journal since 1995 with three issues a year. 🕸
- **Annual review of sociology online**.
  (address – http://198.94.213/soc/home.htm).
  Abstracts of articles published in the *Annual review of sociology* since 1985. Articles in full-text since 1993 can be downloaded for a small charge. 🕸
- **Social research UPDATE**.
  (address – www.soc.surrey.ac.uk/).
  A quarterly publication from the University of Surrey. 🕸

Theory and methodology

- **CTHEORY**.
  (address – www.ctheory.com/).
  A journal of theory, technology and culture, with a strong bias towards Jean Baudrillard. ⬟
- **Social research update**.
  (address – www.soc.surrey.ac.uk/sru/Sru.html).
  From the Department of Sociology at the University of Surrey, this has a focus on developing new methods in relation to information communications technology. ⬟
- **The qualitative report**.
  (address – www.nova.edu/sss/QR/index.html).
  A peer-reviewed online journal dedicated to qualitative and critical inquiry. ⬟

JOURNAL (SERIALS) SERVICES AND SEARCH SERVICES

Some publishers, like Blackwell and MCB University Press, have journal and article search services. These are mostly fee based and are therefore normally available from libraries subscribing to those services. Although some are aimed at librarians they are sometimes available for students who want to locate journals and relevant articles. Some of the main services are as follows.

- **Serials connect on the world wide web**.
  (address – http://serialsconect.blackwell.co.uk/).
  Link to Blackwell's database of serials and serials information including ISSNs, titles, editors, URL details, links between series and information on electronic publications. ⬟ ☎
- **Blackwell's electronic journal navigator**.
  Extensive searching and browsing facilities across a substantial number of electronic journal collections. ⬟ ☎
- **UnCover**.
  (address – http://uncweb.carl.org/).
  Indexing service for over 18,000 journal titles with over eight million article citations makes this a powerful service. ⬟ ☎
- **OCLC First search**.
  Online computer library centre that provides access to over 85 databases, 6,000 periodicals (some full-text), images, and catalogues of other libraries including the Library of Congress. Many of the core indexes and abstracts for the social sciences, arts and humanities and medical sciences are included such as *Arts & humanities search*, *Periodical contents index*, *PsychINFO*, *Sociological abstracts* and many more. ⬟ ☎

- **NISS EBSCO**.
  NISS EBSCO MasterFILE service provides access to indexing and abstracting of 3,100 academic journals, some full text, along with many databases such as *ERIC*, *PsychLIT* and *Sociofile*. 🕸 ☎ ⊙
- **Emerald intelligence and full-text**.
  (address – www.mcb.co.uk/emerald.htm).
  This electronic management research library database searches and retrieves articles from the top 100 management journals dating back to 1989. 🕸 ☎

CURRENT AWARENESS SERVICES

If you are doing a project that will take a year or more then you will need to keep informed about any recent publications. To keep a *watching brief* use current awareness services along with the core indexes and abstracting services for your topic. Current awareness services will alert you to articles that have recently been, or are about to be, published. Most are fee or subscription based. Depending on the topic, some are published weekly and others monthly. They reproduce the contents pages of journals published in a given period for a given topic. In this way the reader can scan the contents of large numbers of journals. Such browsing activities are a way of keeping up with the literature rather than an effective tool for searching for relevant items. However, as more current content services become available in electronic format they will become more useful as a searching tool. Along with the following, most major academic publishers provide an alerting service.

- **Current contents: arts and humanities**.
  Philadelphia: Institute for Scientific Information. ⊙ ☎
- **Current contents: social and behavioral sciences**.
  Philadelphia: Institute for Scientific Information. Also available online as Current contents search through KRI. 📖 ☎
- **Inside information on CD ROM**.
  Boston Spa: BLDSC. ⊙
- **Regard**.
  (address – www.regard.ac.uk/).
  Free from the ESRC UK: contains details of research projects they fund with links to research sites.
- **UnCover**.
  (address – http://uncweb.carl.org/reveal/).
  Blackwell's electronic current awareness alerting service provides current information on any or all of 18,000 titles.
- **Inside**.
  (address – www.bl.uk/online/inside/).

British Library alerting service that allows you to search the BL's journal and conference collections.

SUMMARY OF THIS CHAPTER

- Articles from refereed journals (print and electronic) are an essential source of information and knowledge for all students and researchers.
- Indexing and abstracting services provide the means to search for relevant articles.
- Citation indexes will help you to find the source of an idea, theory or study.

7

Finding grey literature

This chapter will show you:

- how to find theses and dissertations
- how to find magazines and newspaper articles
- how to find what research is in progress
- how to find film, video, music, art work and images
- how to find alternative literature and fan literature

A range of published and unpublished material which is not normally identifiable through conventional methods of bibliographic control (e.g. ISBNs and ISSNs) is called grey literature. The types of material included in this category are – theses undertaken for higher degrees, papers and speeches given at conferences, notices of research in progress, newspaper articles and editorials, personal diaries and letters, materials produced by businesses such as trade catalogues and advertisements, leaflets and posters, and other types of ephemera including objects commemorating an event, web sites, virtual discussions, and publications by clubs. From this list you can see that a large amount of material comes into this category and due to the lack of bibliographical controls it is sometimes difficult to identify and obtain. Figure 7.1 provides an overview of the types of material that are normally classified as grey literature.

There are ways, however, to identify and locate many types of grey literature and what we will focus on is grey literature relevant to research in the social sciences, arts and humanities. This means we will not look at reports from business, trade literature or personal correspondence. Some local authorities, for example, collect and archive material used by candidates standing for election. This type of collection could be very useful to a number of

Tip: archives often contain a substantial amount of grey literature. Use guides to archives, special libraries and museums to see if there is a collection relevant to your topic.

scholars. Many local and county authorities have local studies collections and extensive archives that house material relating to the region and the people who have lived in it. The relevance of special collections in local archives should not be overlooked, especially when researching significant persons, places, movements or industries. Regrettably this is not the place

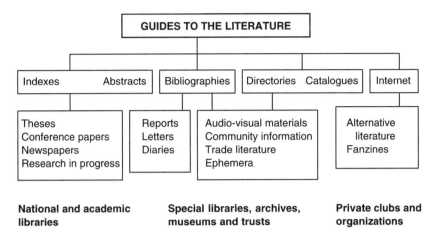

Figure 7.1 *The bibliographical framework for grey literature*

to look in detail at archival sources and their use. The references that follow are indicative only and should be supplemented with a search for literature relevant to using archives.

GUIDES TO THE LITERATURE

- **Information sources in grey literature**.
  4th edn. Auger, C.P. London: Bowker-Saur, 1998. 📖
- **System for grey literature in Europe (SIGLE)**.
  Substantial international set of databases which arrange grey literature by subject content. Produced by the European Association for Grey Literature (EAGLE). All EU member countries are included. The data-bases have information since 1980 on reports, theses and dissertations, conferences, academic materials and miscellaneous. The databases are categorized into social sciences and humanities, technology, natural sciences and biology and medicine. Access is available through BlaiseLine from the British Library (address – http://portico.bl.uk/dsc/) and the Office of Official Publications of the European Communities. Some central regional libraries such as Birmingham Public Library have European documentation centres that can also provide access and will have copies of a user guide to SIGLE. The databases are also available from SilverPlatter on CD ROM. 📘 ⊙ 🕸 ☎
- **Grey Net**.
  (address – www.konbib.nl/infolev/greynet/).
  The Grey Literature Network Service established in the Netherlands in 1992, now a branch of MCB Press, is an ongoing compilation of different topic-based bibliographies on grey literature and guides to organizations and persons related to grey literature. 🕸 ☎

- **Collection building**.
  This is a reputable journal that often contains articles on interesting and useful collections of materials from around the world.

Along with a number of university libraries, such as the University of Reading, the British Library is now collecting grey literature and ephemera. Remember to check if your university library has a collection of grey literature and ephemera.

FINDING THESES

Theses completed for successful PhDs can be a very important source of recent original work. They are also a useful source of bibliographical references. The major way to search for relevant theses is by consulting the following:

- **ASLIB index to theses**.
  ASLIB. Published quarterly, it covers theses from UK universities and higher education institutes. It includes full abstracts and is arranged by subject and author. 📑 🏯
- **Dissertation abstracts international**
  UMI. Mainly a source on North American theses, it is arranged in broad subject categories including the social sciences. 📑 ☉ ☎
- **Retrospective index to theses in Great Britain and Ireland 1716–1950**.
  A comprehensive multi-set volume indexing theses accepted before 1950. 📑

The major problem with theses is that in the UK, unlike the USA, there is lack of a reliable and systematic procedure for providing copies of theses. Successful doctoral work is not always indexed by the major indexes and abstracts and the British Library does not always collect or receive a copy of the thesis. Availability of theses is variable, but remember that they are normally made available on microfiche. The British Library Document Supply Centre and the University of London, however, have substantial collections of theses and together they index many thousands of new ones each year.

FINDING CONFERENCE PAPERS

If you need to have a 'state of the art' search then a search for conference materials will be essential. The proceedings of conferences can be searched using the following sources:

- **Index of conferences proceedings received**.
  Boston Spa: BLDSC. This is published monthly. *Boston Spa conferences on CD-ROM* does not index individual papers, only the titles of conferences. 📖 ☉ ☎
- **Inside conferences on CD-ROM**.
  Boston Spa: BLDSC. Available since 1994, this indexes papers of the 15,000 conference proceedings received by BLDSC. ☉
- **Index to social and humanities proceedings**.
  ISI. This international index of conferences indexes over 21,000 individual papers and can be searched using key words, author and location. ☉ ☎
- **Proceedings: BUBL Link**.
  (address – http://bubl.ac.uk/link/types/proceedings.htm).
  A section of BUBL with a range of links to conference material. 🕸
- **The directory of scholarly and professional e-conferences**.
  (address – www.n2h2.com/KOVACS/html).
  Internet version of the Association of Research Libraries, *Directory of electronic journals, newsletters and academic discussion lists*. An A–Z directory of scholarly and professional e-conferences, discussion lists, and more. 🕸

Most professional associations like the British Sociological Association and British Psychological Association hold annual and special conferences on current subjects and issues. To find out what conferences are forthcoming and which have taken place contact the associations relevant to your topic. You will normally be able to obtain, for a small charge, a copy of papers given at past conferences.

> **Tip:** *use yearbooks to find details on associations.*

FINDING MAGAZINES AND NEWS PUBLICATIONS

Many thousands of different popular magazines, periodicals and newspapers are published each week (for scholarly journals – see Chapter 6). Examples include *The Guardian*, *The Times*, *The Economist*. Since the late 1980s many periodicals and newspapers have been indexed and are increasingly available in full-text on CD ROM and online. Many popular magazines and newspapers will contain materials that might have relevance to your research topic: for instance analysis of key issues and interviews with key players in an event. There is a range of guides to periodicals, magazines and newspapers but sometimes obtaining an article from an issue of a popular magazine can be difficult.

> **Tip:** *use the quick reference section of the library to find sources listed in this section (see Chapter 4).*

Guides to magazine titles

- **Willings press guide**.
  East Grinstead: British Media Publications, 1871—. 📖
- **Magazines for libraries**.
  Bowker-Saur: Katz, B. and Katz, L. (eds) regular updates. 📖 ⊙ 🏯
- **Magazine listings: BUBL**.
  (address – http://bubl.ac.uk/link/types/magazines.htm).
  A growing list of links to magazine listings and sources. 🏯
- **Ulrich's international periodicals directory**.
  Bowker-Saur, regularly updated. CD ROM and online versions
  (**Ulrichsweb.com**) have links to indexes, document ordering services
  and evaluations. ⊙ 📖 ☎
- **General periodicals index/ASAP**.
  Gale: general reference source of a vast array of titles both academic
  and general, including newspapers, with a growing number of full-text
  articles. ⊙
- **Periodical contents index**.
  Chadwyck-Healey: provides access to contents pages of over 2,750
  titles and records for over 10 million articles since the eighteenth
  century. ⊙ ☎
- **The Wellesley index to Victorian periodicals 1824–1900**.
  Routledge: provides an index to 43 nineteenth century British
  periodicals. ⊙

To find *links to the publishers* of specific titles consult the following type of
gateway:

- **Galileo**.
  (address – www.usg.edu/galileo.html).
  Links to a wide range of international magazines including *Ecola
  Newsstand* and *NewLink's Magazines Directory*.
- **Digital librarian**.
  (address – www.servtech.com/).
  A long list of magazine links and sources.

Finding and searching newspapers

There are now some comprehensive indexes to newspapers and the British
Library has a Newspaper Library that can give you access to a range of
full-text CD ROMs and fiche copies of the newspapers themselves.

- **British newspaper index**.
  Primary Source Media: electronic index of ten British quality newspapers that is updated monthly. ⊙

- **Newspaper abstracts**.
  Bell & Howell Information: abstracts and index to US newspapers since 1989. ⊙
- **Newspapers and business information**.
  Chadwyck-Healey: collection of British quality newspapers on CD ROM including *The Times Higher Educational Supplement*. ⊙ ☎
- **Palmer's full-text online 1785–1870/1905**.
  Chadwyck-Healey: fully searchable index to *The Times* with full-text articles. ⊙ ☎
- **The British Library Newspaper Library**.
  (address – www.bl.uk/collections/newspapers/).
  National archive collection of newspapers at the British Library. ⊙ 🕸

FINDING RESEARCH IN PROGRESS

There are thousands of research centres and universities around the world undertaking all types of research. If you are doing a PhD it can be very useful to find out who is doing research on your topic so that you can contact them,

> **Tip:** *remember that most gateways have a listing of research centres.*

ask their advice and inform them of what you are doing. To find out if there is a research centre on your topic or if anyone else is doing work, say for a PhD, related to your topic consult the following:

- **Research centres and services directory**.
  Gale: covers nearly 13,800 university-related and independent not-for-profit research organizations in the US and Canada. ☎ 🕸
- **Current research in Britain**.
  British Library: a detailed directory of information on research being undertaken in Britain. 📖 ⊙ ☎
- **Internet research registers**.
  (address – www.mcb.co.uk.literi/research_registers/).
  MCB Press: a voluntary register set up by a commercial publisher. 🕸
- **SocioSite: research centres**.
  (address – www.pscw.uva.nl/sociosite.html).
  Provides links to research centres worldwide. 🕸

FINDING AUDIO-VISUAL MATERIALS

Audio-visual materials do not usually include critical discussion or analysis but they can provide the primary source on which many researchers based their work. The following list is an indicative guide to film, video, art, music and image (e.g. photograph and poster) sources which fall within our definition of grey literature.

> **Tip:** *remember that guides to the literature (see Chapter 4) will provide references to commercially produced indexes on film, music and video.*

Finding film, video materials and reviews

There are many general sources for film (i.e. cinema) on the Internet which can be found via most general search engines (e.g. Yahoo) and specialist search engines (e.g. CHOICE) but for more authoritative sources consult the following:

- **The complete index to film since 1895**.
  Bowker-Saur: searchable by title, director, actors, place and more. ⊙
- **Film index international**.
  British Film Institute/Chadwyck-Healey: a two-database disk on films and personalities since 1930. ⊙
- **Video directory on disc**.
  Bowker-Saur: over 100,000 titles, including 58,000 educational titles and documentaries. ⊙
- **The Internet movie database**.
  (address – www.imdb.com/).
  Large database dedicated to cinema. 🏛
- **WebSEEK**.
  (address – www.crt.columbia.edu/webseek/).
  A content-based image and video searchable catalogue that aims to index visual materials on the Internet.

Finding art and art criticism

Information technology has made an incredible amount of art available via digitization on CD ROM and via the Internet. Several indexes are regularly produced, along with some excellent services from art galleries and museums worldwide.

- **Art abstracts**.
  Wilson: covers over 370 periodicals with indexing back to 1984 and abstracting to 1994. Also **Art full-text** (Wilson) provides full-text articles and information from relevant yearbooks and some museum bulletins. Coverage includes advertising, photography and graphic art. ⊙
- **Art retrospective**.
  Wilson: coverage from 1929 to 1984 with index of reproductions to aid locating copies. ⊙
- **Grove dictionary of art**.
  One of several reference sources on art from Macmillan. Contains articles, research and bibliographical citations with links to museums, galleries and art sites around the world. 📖 ⊙ ☎

Most academic gateways (e.g. Digital Librarian, CHOICE, SocioSite) have listings and links to Internet art sources and resources. For details see the following:

- **ADAM**.
  (address – http://adam.ac.uk/).
  Art, Design, Architecture & Media Information gateway that provides a wide range of links to quality sources arranged by category, e.g. fine arts, theory and practice. 🕸
- **Arts and humanities data service**.
  (address – http://ahds.ac.uk/).
  UK resource base for electronic sources in the humanities. Includes a category 'Visual arts and data' that gives access to a wide range of source materials including the Imperial War Museum art collection. 🕸
- **HUMBUL**.
  (address – http://info.ox.ac.uk/oucs/humanities/international.html).
  A selective list to a range of art resources including ADAM, art history, museums and specific collections. 🕸
- **Galileo**.
  (address – www.usg.edu/galileo.html).
  A well organized set of quality links to sources and resources categorized as general resources, art history, images, museums, dictionaries, indexes, journals, libraries, academic departments and organizations. 🕸
- **FineArt forum resource directory**.
  (address – www.msstate.edu.html).
  A long A–Z listing of art resources and sources. 🕸
- **Voice of the shuttle**.
  (address – http://vos.ucsb.edu/shuttle.html).
  A substantial listing of links to art and art history arranged in 11 categories including art theory. 🕸
- **BIOTN: art and architecture**.
  (address – www.squ.edu/bestinfo/pictures/pixindex.htm).
  Hand-picked links to art sites.

Finding music collections

All kinds of music and associated information can be located on the Internet and from specialist libraries. In the UK music libraries are now on a network (*Music online*) enabling their catalogues to be searched.

- **OCLC music library**.
  Provides information on recordings, works and artists, with over 800,000 citations. ☉
- **National sound archive**.
  British Library: a broad-based archive of sounds and music including oral history recordings. Expert advice available from librarians.
- **Voice of the shuttle**.
  (address – http://vos.ucsb.edu/shuttle/).

Links to music and dance resources arranged into categories including general resources, non-western music, theory, dance and zines. ✿

- **WebGEMS**.
  (address – www.fpsol.com/gems.html).
  Links to resources for music, dance and theatre. ✿
- **Librarian's index to the Internet**.
  (address – http://lii.org/).
  Well organized set of links to resources on music categorized as *best of*, *directories*, and *specific resources*. ✿
- **Digital librarian**.
  (address – www.servtech.com/).
  Long list of resources arranged A–Z. ✿

Finding image collections

The numerous picture libraries and image collections now available provide access to millions of pictures, many on CD ROM and the Internet.

For guides to *picture libraries* and collections consult the following:

- **The picture researcher's handbook**.
  Evans, H., Evans, M. and Nelki, A. London: David & Charles, 1975.
  Still a major source on picture libraries and collections. 📖
- **British Association of Picture Libraries (BAPLA)**.
  13 Woodberry Crescent, London, N10 1PJ.
  Association of picture libraries that has a regular journal.

The main guide to finding *images on the Internet* is:

- **Finding images online**.
  Wilton, C.T. Pemberton Books, 1996.
  A dated but still useful and detailed source for finding images on the Internet. 📖

On the Internet the following are useful *sources for finding images*:

- **Librarian's index to the Internet**.
  (address – http://lii.org/).
  Links to most of the major search engines and sources for images, directories, databases and specific resources (also see Lii's *Graphics* category). ✿
- **Image finder**.
  (address – http://sunsite.berkeley.edu/).
  Allows you to search 13 major image databases. ✿
- **Corbis pictures on the Internet**.
  Bill Gates' picture corporation Corbis collects and sells images, with over 500,000 for viewing. ✿

- **Arts and humanities data service**.
  (address – http://ahds.ac.uk/).
  UK resource base for electronic sources in the humanities. Includes links to digital image collections. ✿
- **WebGEMS**.
  (address – www.fpsol.com/gems/).
  A list of quality links to some excellent image and art collections including the Getty databases and images from medieval manuscripts and Victorian publications. ✿
- **Cartoons**.
  There are many interesting collections such as this (available from MicroInformation) – a collection of cartoons published in British newspapers between 1912 and 1990. Also consult the Centre for the Study of Cartoons and caricature based at the University of Kent, Canterbury. ☉
- **René Wanner's poster page**.
  (address – www.datacomm.ch/~wanner/pbookm.htm).
  Links to many sites on posters and poster design.
- **European poster collections**.
  (address – http://freia.dei.unipd.it/poster/pagine/epocgerman.html).
  Information (in German) on posters 1914–45.

FINDING ALTERNATIVE LITERATURE

A growing body of literature published for non-commercial reasons by persons wanting to focus attention on 'social responsibility' or an 'issue' is often called alternative literature. Publications by some organizations such as Amnesty International are relatively well known and are often available in public libraries. The publications of other organizations such as Campaign Against the Arms Trade tend not to be so well known. Alternative literature often gives us a different view on an issue or topic, helping us to develop our critical capacities. There are no authoritative guides to alternative literature but there are some ways of finding out if any exists that is relevant to your topic.

- **Alternative literature: a practical guide for librarians**.
  Atton, C. Aldershot: Gower, 1996. Informed and useful book from an author who knows the subject domain very well. 📖
- **WebGEMS**.
  (address – www.fpsol.com/gems/).
  Links to sites on social issues, e.g. hate groups on the Internet, civil liberties and homelessness. ✿
- **SocioSite**.
  (address – www.pscw.uva.nl/sociosite/).

A well organized set of links to social movements, newsgroups and reference sources. 🕸

- **San Francisco Whole Earth Lectronic Link (The WELL)**.
  (address – www.sbu.ac.uk/guides/eegtti/eeg_131.html).
  An Internet directory to which anyone can send an entry. 🕸
- **DisInformation**.
  (www.disinfo.com/).
  Uses the slogan 'information is power' to provide alternative views on corporate culture.

Although not strictly alternative literature, there is a growing number of sites with a political or moral standpoint. Some of the more useful and semi-official have attracted attention and are seen as having historical value. Look for material such as the following for interpretations and argument on the value of grey literature in given areas:

- 'Grey literature is a feminist issue: women's knowledge and the net'. Malina, D. and Nutt, D. *International Journal on Grey Literature*, 1 (1), 2000, www.emerald-library.com/brev/24601ac1.htm).

FINDING FAN LITERATURE

Groups of people all around the world have a shared interest in something, such as a pop group (e.g. the Beatles), an object (e.g. HMS *Hood*), a person (e.g. Greer Garson), a team (e.g. Manchester United) and many other

> **Tip:** *this literature is an ever changing domain, so look for discussion groups and mailing lists.*

things. They often share information via fan magazines – fan*zines* – that they publish and distribute to members of the club or association. Fanzines contain both factual information and critical evaluations of their topic. For example, fan sites on Jane Austen are often indistinguishable from commercially and professionally published directories and encyclopaedias. These contain a massive amount of information not available anywhere else. Many fanzines are now published on the Internet. If your topic is in the area of popular culture, literature, film studies, art or history then there is probably a fan site on your topic. Knowing the bibliographical structure of the literature (see Figure 7.2) should help you to undertake a search for fan information. The main listing of electronic fanzines is

- **E-Zine**.
  (address – www.meer.net/~johnl/e-zine-list/index.html).
  John Labovitz's list of over 4,000 electronic zines around the world. 🕸

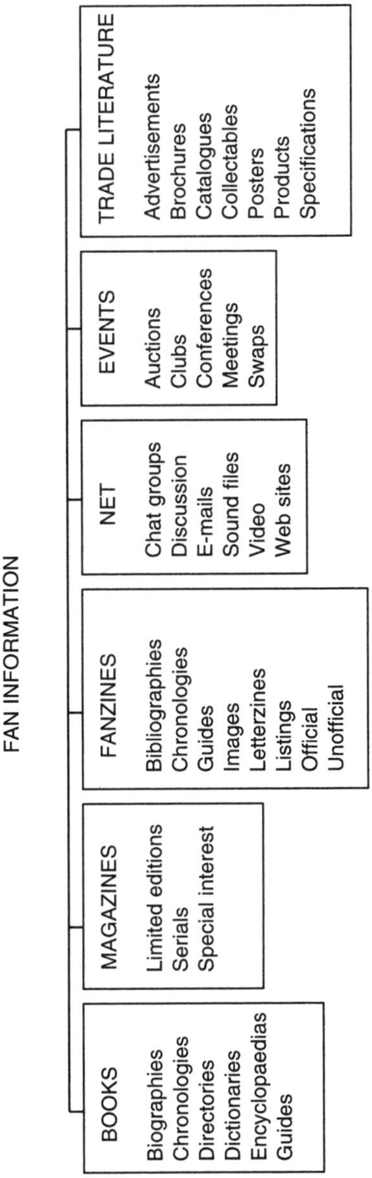

FAN INFORMATION

BOOKS	MAGAZINES	FANZINES	NET	EVENTS	TRADE LITERATURE
Biographies	Limited editions	Bibliographies	Chat groups	Auctions	Advertisements
Chronologies	Serials	Chronologies	Discussion	Clubs	Brochures
Directories	Special interest	Guides	E-mails	Conferences	Catalogues
Dictionaries		Images	Sound files	Meetings	Collectables
Encyclopaedias		Letterzines	Video	Swaps	Posters
Guides		Listings	Web sites		Products
		Official			Specifications
		Unofficial			

Figure 7.2 *The bibliographical structure of fan information*

SUMMARY OF THIS CHAPTER

- An increasing amount of information is being published outside of conventional bibliographical control and by non-commercial publishers. Some of it can form the basis of evaluation, review and alternative perspectives for your own research.
- Many doctoral theses are not published yet contain substantial amounts of information, analysis and knowledge, including bibliographies and reviews of the literature.
- Recent and forthcoming conferences will provide current thinking and research on a topic.
- Audio-visual materials are not a literature but are often the topic for the literature, so obtaining a copy of the original used in your topic is very useful.
- Pressure groups often publish materials that give an alternative view, offering an additional perspective on your topic.
- The majority of people who contribute to fanzines are well informed, and provide information and critical analysis of their topic which can help you identify current issues and people to talk to about your topic.

8

Finding official publications, statistics and archives

This chapter will show you:

- how to find government publications
- how to find statistical sources
- how to find archives and archived data

Official and government publications, statistics and archives can be key sources of data, information and materials for analysis. Reports on social problems, Parliamentary debates on issues of the day, statistics on the occurrences of a type of behaviour, and historic documents on an event are often used as sources by many studies in the social sciences and humanities. Identifying official publications and accessible archives can be difficult because of the vast range of organizations and bodies that issue 'official' publications and have collections of data and other archived materials. This chapter takes each of these three types of material and shows you how to search for items that may be relevant to your research topic.

FINDING OFFICIAL PUBLICATIONS

Understanding the range and nature of official and non-official government publications will help you to find what you are looking for more efficiently and with greater accuracy. The following kinds of publication provide guides to the range and structure of official and other government publications:

- **Official publications in Britain**.
  Butcher, D. London: Bingley, 1991. 📖
- **Information sources in official publications**.
  Nurcombe, V.J. (ed.). London: Bowker-Saur, 1997. 📖
- **Who publishes information on health, safety and social services?**
  London: Library Association, Information Services Group, 1989. 📖

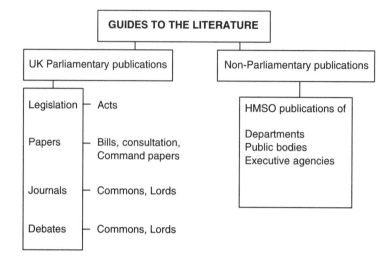

Figure 8.1   *The bibliographical framework for official publications*

To locate a publication on a topic related to government and politics, consult the following general databases:

- **UKOP** *VersionII*.
  (address – www.ukop.co.uk/).
  Chadwyck-Healey. Provides access to the latest information from and on the British governments (e.g. England, Scotland, Wales and Northern Ireland). A combination of the *Catalogue of the Stationery Office and Catalogue of British publications not published by HMSO*, it is updated daily with the latest government publications from over 400 organizations with links to full-text documents when they are available. 🕸 ☎

- **PAIS**.
  Public Affairs Information Service. A service indexing over 1,600 journals and 8,000 monographs annually, including yearbooks and directories. Coverage is wide and includes government, health, international relations, labour and public policy, with an emphasis on factual and statistical information. Available on disk and through *Dialog* and *Datastar*. ⊙ ☎

- **Official documents**.
  (address – www.official-documents.co.uk/).
  From The Stationery Office. Designed to help people locate official documents. 🕸

Internet sources on official publications and governments

A growing number of Internet resources and sources provide an incredible amount of detail on government in the UK and worldwide. The major multi-subject gateways all have sections on government and politics. For a *general search* consult the following:

- **SOSIG.**
  (address – www.sosig.ac.uk/).
- **Librarian's index to the Internet.**
  (address – http://lii.org/).
- **Digital librarian.**
  (address – www.servtech.com/).

For sources on *British government and politics* consult the following:

- **BUBL: Government links** and **Political science: general resources.**
  (address – www.bubl.ac.uk/).
  Government links provides links to a number of lengthy guides to government publications, political fact sources and biographical sources on world politicians. *Political science: general resources* provides links to some major historic archives on British politics and government such as the British Library of Political and Economic Science (BLPES). 🖔
- **Governments online.**
  (address – http://europa.eu.int/gonline_en.html).
  A gateway to online sources for European governments. For the UK it has links to the Foreign and Commonwealth Office, Number 10 Downing Street and the government information service that provides links to web sites on many aspects of public life in Britain, from central government departments to local councils and non-government organizations. 🖔
- **The Keele guides to government and politics on the Internet.**
  (address – www.keele.ac.uk/depts/por/ukbase.html).
  A gateway to a substantial range of sources and resources on UK government and related issues, including all government departments, MI5, *Inforoute* (gateway to official UK information from HMSO), security service records 1914–45, a spy list, the Public Record Office and links to social movements, campaigns and protest groups. 🖔
- **BOPCAS.**
  (address – www.soton.ac.uk/~bopcas/).
  British Official Publication Current Awareness Service. Database of UK official publications. 🖔

FINDING STATISTICS

Many publications include statistical data in support of their argument and in some cases the publication is about what data has been collected. It is therefore important to

> **Tip:** *remember that yearbooks, almanacs and directories also give statistics. See Chapter 4 for more details.*

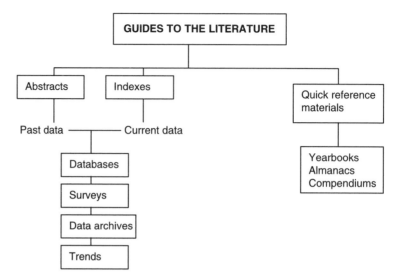

Figure 8.2   *The bibliographical framework for statistical sources*

know what data are available and how to evaluate the data others present as evidence in support of their work. Figure 8.2 gives an overview of the bibliographical framework for statistical data.

Reference sources for locating statistics

Resources for locating statistical data include indexes, abstracts, yearbooks, almanacs and other compendiums of facts. The following are some of the main routes to British and European statistics.

UK and European (EU) statistics
- **Guide to official statistics**.
  Office for National Statistics. Invaluable reference for tracing primary sources of statistics on a very wide range of topics. ⊙ 🕸 📖
- **Annual abstract of statistics**.
- **Monthly digest of statistics**.
  Office for National Statistics. These two publications are the main indexing and abstracting services for UK statistics on a wide range of topics. The *Abstract* has been published for over 140 years and is a comprehensive collection of data about the UK. It is easy to use and has explanatory notes and definitions. The *Digest* provides monthly and quarterly data with updates. ▉ ⊙

The National Statistics Service, along with other organizations, produces regular catalogues of statistical sources. Here are some of the main services that have catalogues.

UK and European sources for statistics

- **National Statistics Service**.
  (address – www.emap.co.uk/ons and www.ons.gov.uk/).
  The major source for statistical data on the UK. Produces a comprehensive catalogue of publications covering the economy, health, labour markets, manufacturing, population, regions, service sector industries and society in general. Publishes the main reference sources along with some very useful guides for students and researchers. ▤ ☉ ⬟

- **StatBase: official statistics online**.
  (address – www.statistics.gov.uk/).
  Made up of two components: *StatSearch* – a free catalogue listing the latest Government Statistic Service (GSS) products and services, providing details of primary sources, analysis and contact points; and *StatStore* – a database of key economic and social statistics. ☉ ⬟

- **Eurostat**.
  (address – http://euroa.eu.int/eurostat.html).
  With more than 18 million enterprises and 110 million people Eurostat publicizes the statistical data of the European Union. Some data are available online but are nearly always available from the regional European Documentation Centre. ▤ ☉ ⬟

- **SubNatStats: a subject index to sub-national statistics**.
  Fitches, J. and Grove, I. London: London Research Centre, 1999.
  An index of statistics from 191 publications.

There are several regular publications of useful statistics which normally have some statistics on all major topics:

- **Social trends**.
  Office for National Statistics. Annual publication which presents the main social and economic data in a user-friendly format. Includes articles and explanations. ▥ ☉

- **25 years of social trends**.
  Office for National Statistics. Survey of British society from 1970 covering a wide range of changes. Data are drawn from a range of government departments. ☉

- **Regional trends**.
  Office for National Statistics. Comprehensive annual source of statistics on the regions of Britain. ▥ ☉

- **Census**.
  London: HMSO. There are several publications providing a massive amount of data from the decennial censuses, e.g. *1991 census: key statistics series*. ▥ ☉

- **The general household survey**.
  London: Office for National Statistics. This survey produced several publications, such as *Living in Britain*, a comprehensive picture of how we live and the social change experienced in Britain. ▥ ☉

Other useful publications that have *guides* to statistical sources include the following:

- **Population statistics: a review of UK sources**.
  Benjamin, B. Aldershot: Gower, 1989. A guide to the range of sources on population data, covering fertility, mortality, marriage and divorce, health, censuses and surveys, migration, longitudinal studies, and more. 📖
- **The societies of Europe: historical data handbook series**.
  London: Macmillan. Flora, P., Kraus, F. and Rothenbacher, F. (eds). Series of reference sources each covering a topic, e.g. elections 1815–1995, trade unions since 1945 and social security systems. Each book comes with a CD ROM with tables and documentation not included in the book. 📖
- **Britain 1999: the official yearbook of the UK**.
  In-depth and up-to-date reference with wide coverage of every aspect of life in Britain. 📖
- **Plain figures**.
  Office for National Statistics. From the Civil Service College, this shows the ways that statistics ought to be used. 📖

FINDING ARCHIVES INCLUDING DATA ARCHIVES

There are many thousands of archives with substantial collections of text documents, illustrations and data. Collections can be found in public records offices, local libraries and local history collections, universities, museums, trusts, companies and in private hands. If you need to look at primary source materials from the past, then an archive might exist with useful materials. Figure 8.3 gives an overview of the bibliographical framework for archives.

> **Tip:** *remember that some data archives are available online and via the Internet (see Chapter 10).*

Finding archives

A number of regularly published reference sources offer a listing and guide to UK and international archives and special collections. Consult the first set of sources to see if an archive exists on your topic and consult the second set to see if there are any relevant data archives on your topic.

Archives and special collections   The following kind of publication lists the main archives and special collections in the UK and Europe:

- **British archives: a guide to archive resources in the United Kingdom**.
  Foster, J. and Sheppard, J. (eds). London: Macmillan, 1999. 📖
- **A directory of rare books and special collections in the United Kingdom and the Republic of Ireland**.
  Bloomfield, B.C. (ed.). London: Library Association, 1999. 📖

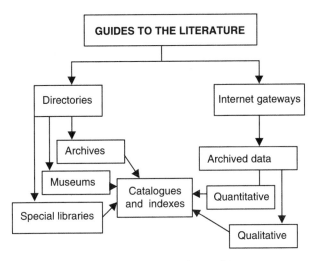

Figure 8.3   *The bibliographical framework for archive sources*

- **Libraries in the United Kingdom and the Republic of Ireland 2000.**
  London: Library Association, 1999. 📖
- **Directory of special libraries in Western Europe.**
  Gallico, A. London: Bowker-Saur, 1993. 📖 ☎

Data archives   The following sources have links to data archives world-wide:

- **SocioSite: social science data archives.**
  (address – www.pscw.uva.nl/sociosite/).
  Categorizes data archives according to broad geographic regions. 🕸
- **World wide web virtual library: social sciences directories and data archives.**
  (address – www.clas.ufl.edu/users/).
  A good list of worldwide data archives. 🕸

Internet sources for archives and data   With the Internet and digitization has come an ever increasing number of archives, data archives and special libraries that are accessible electronically. The following lists some of the major gateways along with specific archive centres. In some cases full text document retrieval is possible but in the main the holding library levies a fee for a copy of any document.
   Useful gateways to archives are

- **Digital librarian: archives and manuscripts.**
  (address – www.servtech.com/).
  Excellent list of sources for locating archives and special collections worldwide with links to specific collections. 🕸

- **Librarian's index to the Internet: museums**.
  (address – www.lii.org/).
  A well indexed and very useful set of links to a selected list (quite long) of directories, databases and specific sites, many of which have special collections. 🕸

Specific examples of archives and specific archives:

- **The data archive**.
  (address – http://155.245.254.47).
  ESRC. The largest store of computer-readable data on the social sciences and humanities in the UK. To access some data sets you need to go through BIRON (Bibliographical Information Retrieval Online). 🕸
- **ESRC Qualitative data archive**.
  (address – www.essex.ac.uk/qualidata/).
  Not a depository but a database service that keeps track of the location of archived qualitative data. The database can be accessed via the QUALICAT search engine. 🕸
- **The history data service**.
  (address – http://hds.essex.ac.uk/homepage.stm).
  Located and integrated with the Data Archive at the University of Essex the archive is accessed through BIRON. Contains about 400 data sets including Census records, community history, statistics for the nineteenth and twentieth centuries and other materials on economic history. 🕸
- **The Noam Chomsky archive**.
  (address – www.worldmedia.com/archive/).
  A substantial collection of materials on and by Chomsky. 🕸
- **Marx and Engels archive**.
  (address – http://cfs.colorado.edu/psn/marx).
  Access to many full-text versions of the writings of Marx and Engels. 🕸
- **The Internet classics archive**.
  (address – http://classics.mit.edu/home/).
  A searchable collection of about 400 Greek and Roman texts translated into English, including works by Plato and Aristotle. 🕸
- **Sources in history: making the United Kingdom**.
  British Library. Provides over 1,000 visual and documentary sources linked to questions such as, 'Was Britain a united kingdom by 1750?' ☉

SUMMARY OF THIS CHAPTER

- A substantial number of official publications are produced by the different spheres of government: these can help you to understand key issues and debates. Most can be located by understanding the types of official publication that exist and by using relevant indexes.

- Statistics are often the basis of research and argument. Methods for evaluating statistics and sources for obtaining them are available through a range of digests and other publications (some on the Internet).
- A large number of archives exist on many topics and issues. These are a useful source for you to use as the basis of your own research.

9

Finding citations and reviews

> This chapter will show you:
>
> - how to use citation indexes to find works related to your topic and the main publications on your topic
> - how to find reviews of books about your topic to help you understand what peer scholars think about work you might use in your research

Citation indexes record the *citations* (references) an author has used in their article or book. If you know the name of a particular author in your topic field then you can search for publications that have cited that author. The indexes (there are several) will list the publications that cite the author and give in alphabetical order other authors also cited. By examining who has been cited you can quickly build up a picture of the main contributors to knowledge on your topic. We will shortly see how this is done. Citation indexes along with other special indexes also provide *reviews* of books. Book reviews are a means to understand how the peers of the author assess that contribution to the topic. The combination of citations and reviews can be an effective means to build up your understanding of the literature, of identifying the major authors, key ideas, theories and concepts and of discovering what empirical work has been done, and what in the literature are considered the primary sources. The general bibliographical framework for citation indexes and review sources is shown in Figure 9.1

CITATION INDEXES

The main citation indexes are provided by the Institute for Scientific Information (ISI) (address – www.isinet.com/). For the social sciences, arts and humanities scholars the following are the most relevant citation indexes available from ISI:

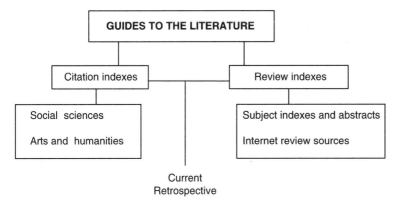

Figure 9.1 *The bibliographical framework for citation indexes and reviews*

- **Social science citation index (SSCI)**.
  Covers 1,700 leading journals in the following disciplines:

Anthropology	Geography	Linguistics
Business	Geriatrics	Philosophy
Communication	Health policy and	Psychiatry
Criminology and	services	Psychology
penology	History	Public health
Economics	Industrial relations	Social issues
Education	and labour law	Social work
Environmental	Information science	Sociology
studies	Language and	Urban studies
Family studies	Political science	Women's studies

  It can be searched using key words, author, cited reference, journal and publisher.
  Updated weekly, it is available from *ISI Web of science*, and through *Dialog* and *Datastar* as **Social SciSearch**. 📖 ☎ ☉

- **Arts and humanities citation index (A&HCI)**.
  Covers 1,140 leading journals in the following disciplines:

Archaeology	Folklore	Philosophy
Architecture	History	Poetry
Art	Language	Radio, television and
Asian studies	Linguistics	film
Classics	Literature	Religion
Dance	Music	Theatre

  It can be searched using key words, author, cited reference, journal and publisher.
  Updated weekly, it is available from *ISI Web of science*, and through *Dialog* and *Datastar* as **Arts & humanities search**. 📖 ☎ ☉

In addition the ISI offers a range of current awareness services for the Arts & humanities and Social & behavioural sciences and an *Index to proceedings, book contents and reviews*. You can also see what journals are the most frequently used or cited by using the *Journal citation reports*.

How do citation indexes work?

To use the citation indexes you normally need to know the name of an author in your topic. For example, if you are trying to find publications about 'popular romance literature' (e.g. the type of books published by Mills & Boon) then Janice Radway, author of *Reading the romance: women, patriarchy, and popular culture* (North Carolina: University of North Carolina Press, 1984; Verso: London, 2nd edn. 1987) is a key author. Her book is a landmark study of romance readers and could be a starting point for finding other publications and authors on the topic, and for assessing the impact Radway has had on understandings of the topic. Any other publication Radway cited will be listed and others who have cited Radway will be also listed.

> **Tip:** *it can take time to teach yourself how to use citation indexes and therefore remember to take detailed notes as you search.*

How to do a citation search and analysis

The ISI citation indexes can be searched and used in a number of ways, as the following screen from ISI shows (Figure 9.2).

From Figure 9.2 you can see that you have a number of options that help you to narrow your search and analyse your results. The seven main options are as follows.

1 Search form for basic key word and author searches.
2 Advanced search form for more detailed searches.
3 Combine or return to any search for your session.
4 Save the set of searches or retrieve, browse or delete previously saved sets.
5 Search for articles that have cited a particular work.
6 Analyse the cited references of articles from a marked list.
7 Select your favourite journals and get the contents of new issues e-mailed to you automatically.

You can also

- display the results of the last successful search;
- display the articles currently in a marked list;
- e-mail results from your search or marked list.

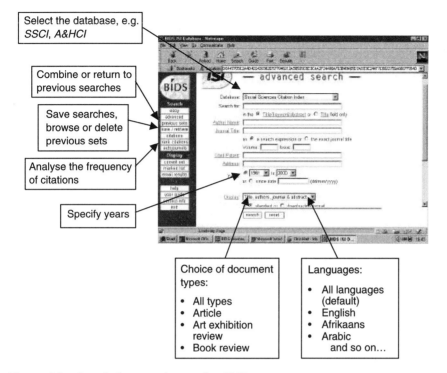

Select the database, e.g. *SSCI, A&HCI*

Combine or return to previous searches

Save searches, browse or delete previous sets

Analyse the frequency of citations

Specify years

Choice of document types:

- All types
- Article
- Art exhibition review
- Book review

Languages:

- All languages (default)
- English
- Afrikaans
- Arabic and so on...

Figure 9.2   *Search form and page for SSCI*

Your search can be limited in three ways:

1   Specify dates for your search, e.g. from 1996 to 1999, remembering that you can be more specific, e.g. 25/3/1990.
2   Specify the document type(s) to be searched, e.g. articles, reviews, etc.
3   Select the language of the documents to be searched and retrieved, e.g. English.

WORKED EXAMPLE: CITATION INDEX USE, *READING THE ROMANCE* (1984)

Using the example of Radway's *Reading the romance* (1984) we can illustrate how citation indexes show relationships between publications and the impact a particular publication may have had on the subsequent development of the topic.

We have begun by entering *Radway_JA* to see what Janice Radway has written other than *Reading the romance* (1984). Figure 9.3 shows what SSCI retrieved for us. If we

> **Tip:** *remember to enter author names as follows: surname_initials, e.g. Radway_JA*

Author	Year	Volume	Page	Journal	Refs
RADWAY_JA				READING ROMANCE	(19 refs)
RADWAY_JA				READING ROMANCE WOME	(3 refs)
RADWAY_JA	1978	Vol.12	P.94	J POPULAR CULTURE	(1 refs)
RADWAY_JA	1978	Vol.12	P.89	J POPULAR CULTURE	(1 refs)
RADWAY_JA	1978	Vol.12	P.88	J POPULAR CULTURE	(1 refs)
RADWAY_JA	1978	Vol.12	P.96	JPC	(1 refs)
RADWAY_JA	1978	Vol.12	P.88	JPC	(1 refs)
RADWAY_JA	1981			AM Q	(1 refs)
RADWAY_JA	1981	Vol.33	P.140	AM Q	(4 refs)
RADWAY_JA	1983	Vol.60	P.53	FEMINIST STUD	(1 refs)
RADWAY_JA	1983	Vol.9	P.53	FEMINIST STUD	(5 refs)
RADWAY_JA	1983	Vol.5	P.53	FEMINIST STUDIES	(1 refs)
RADWAY_JA	1983	Vol.9	P.53	FEMINIST STUDIES	(1 refs)
RADWAY_JA	1983	Vol.9	P.72	FEMINIST STUDIES	(1 refs)
RADWAY_JA	**1984**			**READING ROMANCE**	**(243 refs)**
RADWAY_JA	1984			READING ROMANCE PATR	(1 refs)
RADWAY_JA	1984		P.21	READING ROMANCE WOME	(1 refs)
RADWAY_JA	1984			READING ROMANCE WOME	(41 refs)
RADWAY_JA	1985			READING ROMANCE	(5 refs)
RADWAY_JA	1985			READING ROMANCE WOME	(2 refs)
RADWAY_JA	1986	Vol.2	P.26	BOOK RES Q	(1 refs)
RADWAY_JA	1986	Vol.2	P.7	BOOK RES Q	(4 refs)
RADWAY_JA	1986	Vol.9	P.93	COMMUNICATION	(7 refs)
RADWAY_JA	1986			READING ROMANCE	(2 refs)
RADWAY_JA	1987			READING ROMANCE	(16 refs)
RADWAY_JA	1991			READING ROMANCE	(15 refs)
RADWAY_JA	1996		P.448	COMMUN THEORY	(1 refs)

Figure 9.3   *List of citing publications for Radway, JA*

had also used the *A&HCI* we would have had some more 'hits'. Note that *Reading the romance* (1984) is on the list. Books can usually be identified by the large number of citations while journal materials (i.e. articles, reviews and editorials) are identifiable by the presence of volume and page number.

We could select all or none of these from the list in Figure 9.3 to look at their full records, e.g. author, title, date, journal, ISSN, abstract (if there is one) and citations. We might, for instance, want to see how Radway has developed her work and, importantly, who she cites as these will be relevant to an understanding of her work.

If we were interested in what others have had to say about *Reading the romance* (1984) then we might have selected to see some **reviews**. Figure 9.4 shows a record of a review.

We can select any or all the items on the list to do a **citation search**. This is a method of searching for published works that have cited a particular piece of work, in this case, *Reading the romance* (1984). To do a citation search fill in the *Citation search form* as shown in Figure 9.5. You need not use all the fields but must include an author. Remember to provide, if possible, dates for the search otherwise the entire database will be searched. If you get too many results only use the 'cited work' field.

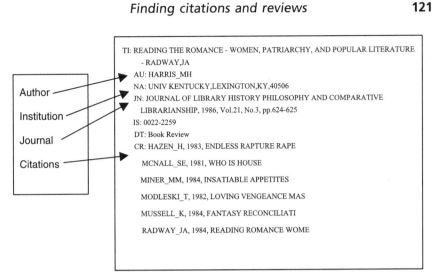

Figure 9.4 *Full record for a book review for 'Reading the romance' (1984)*

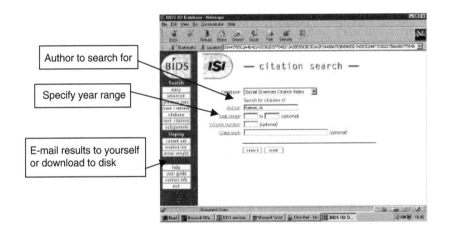

Figure 9.5 *Citation search form*

From the list (as shown in Figure 9.3) you can select any items you would like to look at in more detail. You select items by 'marking' them. Figure 9.6 shows a full record for an author citing *Reading the romance* (1984).

Using the items that we select from the list of those that have cited *Reading the romance* (1984) we can do a **citation analysis**. The citation analysis feature allows you to rank by frequency the authors who have cited a publication. Figure 9.7 shows a citation analysis for *Reading the romance* (1984).

> **Tip:** remember that a citation can be positive – where an author agrees – or negative – where an author criticizes and disagrees with the source they are citing.

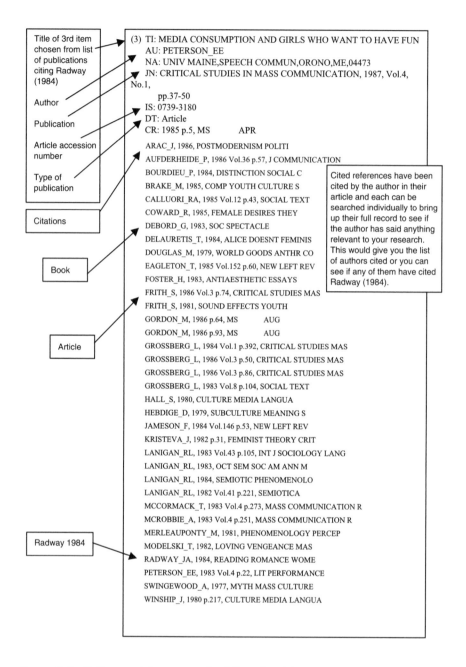

Figure 9.6 *Full record from a marked list of articles citing 'Reading the romance' (1984)*

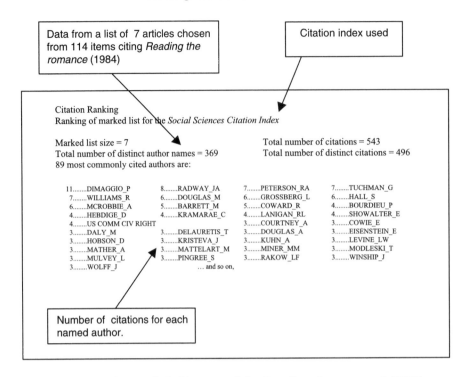

Figure 9.7 *Citation analysis (frequency) for 'Reading the romance' (1984)*

In Figure 9.7 note that the highest frequency is Dimaggio_P. This does not mean that 11 other authors have cited Dimaggio_P. It might be that Dimaggio_P is cited several times in one article, possibly one Dimaggio_P has written. We could check this out by looking at the full record for Dimaggio_P. What we can take from the analysis of frequency is that Radway_JA has 8 citations and may be the second most cited author from the set of seven marked articles. This means that she seems to have had a measurable impact on the topic. We could investigate this by extending the number of marked articles to see what effect this had on Radway_JA's ranking. You could also investigate the working assumption that the others in the frequency have also had an impact on developing the topic. Each could be looked at in turn, and then collectively, to analyse who they have cited, including each other. This analysis could then be represented to plot the relationships between these authors.

Following this brief example you should now be able to see that citation searching consists of three basic stages:

1   the search for references that match the term you have put in the boxes;

2 selection of one or more (or all) the matching references from those retrieved by the database;

3 the retrieval and display of the articles that contain the selected (marked) references.

Tip: *see Chapter 11 for advice on electronic searching and the use of symbols.*

Doing a citation search need not be complex if you follow the instructions given here and online (what you see on the screen). If you are new to citation searching, begin by filling in the boxes and select, if relevant, from the pull-down menus. Remember, however, that citation searching, like other forms of electronic searching, has a search language that employs symbols. Here are the most useful tools for citation searching:

*	is used to truncate a word
?	represents one wild character
#	is used for a wild word in a phrase
+ or &	is used for AND
,	is used for OR
-	is used for NOT

These are called *logical operators*

FINDING REVIEWS

Tip: *remember that many electronic journals publish book reviews.*

Judgements about what to obtain can be helped by looking up reviews of citations for books you have found. The most efficient way of tracing reviews is by using review journals and indexes of reviews. A systematic search of these bibliographical tools will provide reviews that can help you to decide what might be worthy of further pursuit and give you a bank of second opinions. These can be used to help you evaluate a work and aid your selection of materials for inclusion in your literature review. Some of the most useful publications for locating reviews are listed below.

Indexes devoted to reviews

Publications such as the following index the reviews published in a wide range of journals.

- **Book review index**.
  Gale. Wide coverage of topics. ⊙ ▤ ☎
- **Wilson Book review digest**.
  Wilson. Selective indexing of those publications that contain two or more reviews. ⊙ ▤ ☎
- **Index to book reviews in the humanities**.
  Wilmington, Michigan: Thomson. ▤

- **Media review digest**.
  Ann Arbor, Michigan: Pierian Press. ▓

Indexes that include a book review section

Many of the large indexing and abstracting services such as *Sociological Abstracts* index reviews, so search the indexes most relevant to your topic first before searching sources such as the following:

- **American reference books**.
  Littleton, Colorado. ▓
- **Art index**.
  Wilson. 1920. Cumulated annually. ⊙ ▓ ☎
- **Arts and humanities citation index**.
  Institute for Scientific Information. ⊙ ▓ ☎
- **Education index**.
  Wilson. ⊙ ▓ ☎
- **Historical abstracts**.
  Santa Barbara, California, ABC-Clio. ⊙ ▓ ☎
- **Humanities index**.
  Wilson. ⊙ ▓ ☎
- **International index to film periodicals**.
  London, IFFA/International Federation of Film Archives. ⊙ ▓ ☎
- **LLBA/Language and language behavior abstracts**.
  San Diego, California. Sociological Abstracts, Inc. ⊙ ▓ ☎
- **Music index**.
  Detroit, Michigan, Information Co-ordinators. ⊙ ▓ ☎
- **The philosophers' index**.
  Philosophy Documentation Center, Bowling Green State University, Ohio. ⊙ ▓ ☎
- **Serials review**.
  Ann Arbor, Michigan, Pierian Press. ⊙ ▓
- **Social science citation index**.
  Institute for Scientific Information. ⊙ ▓ ☎
- **Social science index**.
  Wilson. ⊙ ▓ ☎

Some retrospective indexes to reviews

- **An author index to selected British 'little magazines', 1930–1939**.
  Bloomfield, Indiana, Barry Cambray. London: Mansell, 1976. ▭
- **Book review index to social science periodicals [1964–74]**.
  Ann Arbor, Michigan: Pierian Press, 1978–80, 4 vols. ▭
- **Combined retrospective index to book reviews in humanities journals, 1802–1974**.
  Woodbridge, Connecticut, RP/Research Publications, 1982–84, 9 vols. (Vols, 1–8, Authors; Vol. 9, Titles). ▭

- **Combined retrospective index to book reviews in scholarly journals, 1886–1974**.
  Woodbridge, Connecticut, RP/Research Publications, 1979, 15 vols. 📖

Internet review sources

There is a growing list of sources available via the Internet to locate reviews. Many are linked to subject disciplines such as psychology and can therefore usually be located using subject listings from the major multi-subject gateways such as BUBL (address – www.bubl.ac.uk/) and WebGEMS (www.fpsol.com/gems/reviews/). Some of the current Internet-based reviewing sources are:

- **Indexes, abstracts, bibliographies, and table of contents**.
  (address – http://info.lib.uh.edu/indexes/indexes.html).
  Subjects covered include sociology, history, philosophy, psychology, political science, gender studies, education, business and economics. Has many links to some substantial bibliographical databases and to the book review databases of the American Psychoanalytic Association. 🕸
- **Australian humanities review**.
  (address – www.lamp.ac.uk/ahr/).
  A review journal started in 1997 that covers a wide range of materials published in the humanities. 🕸
- **H-Net reviews**.
  (address – www.h-net.msu.edu/reviews/).
  Reviews are commissioned by 600+ specialists from around the world who are members of Humanities Net. Searchable by author, title, publisher, reviewer's name and year, using Library of Congress subject classification. 🕸
- **Boston book review**.
  (address – www.bookwire.com/).
  Electronic and edited version of the print version providing reviews of books in politics, history, and social science. 🕸

SUMMARY OF THIS CHAPTER

- Knowing what impact a publication has had on your topic literature can help you identify relationships and influences in the literature.
- Citation indexes will help you to identify key sources and find out who has used those sources, thereby helping you to identify subsequent publications.
- Reviews of books and other materials will help you to decide what is worth reading and help you to understand the contribution particular books are seen to have made to the development of understanding on your topic.

Part C

USING INFORMATION COMMUNICATIONS TECHNOLOGY: MORE ADVANCED KNOWLEDGE AND TECHNIQUES

10

Using the Internet for literature searching

This chapter will show you:

- opportunities for literature searching on the Internet
- how to search the Internet effectively
- how to choose the search tools you need
- how to stay up to date with the Internet

As more and more information is made available in electronic formats (e.g. CD ROM, Internet and online) you can have access to substantial amounts of knowledge and information that might otherwise have been beyond your reach (in the time you have available or in terms of your budget). However, there are a number of major problems with this development. The first is the sheer size of the Internet: it contains an estimated 5 million web sites with about 800 million publicly available documents, and much more is being added daily. The second is the belief that everything can be found 'on the net'. The Internet is still relatively new and a substantial part of the information on it is not academic or research related; and with addresses changing frequently and sites disappearing it is also unreliable. Added to these is the unorganized nature of information on the Internet. There is no Dewey Decimal Classification scheme or central catalogue into which information is placed and organized, although some search services do use DDC (e.g. *Living Web Virtual Library*) to arrange sources on their site. At present the contents of the Internet consist of an unorganized growing mass of information, and as anyone can publish whatever they like on a web page many pages are irrelevant and do not meet any agreed standard. However, there are serious sites and services that can be very useful to the researcher and Figure 10.1 gives an overview of the uses of the Internet to literature searching and research.

> **Tip:** there is a great deal of jargon, much of it abbreviated, to do with the Internet. See the Glossary for some common terms.

There are many guides to help you understand and exploit the Internet and other electronic sources. Some of those useful for literature searching are listed below:

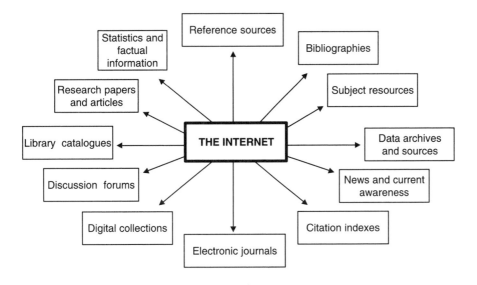

Figure 10.1 *Literature searching opportunities on the Internet*

- **Information seeking in the online age**.
  Large, J.A., Tedd, L.A. and Hartley, R.J. London: Bowker-Saur, 1999. 📖
- **The library and information professional's guide to the Internet**.
  Tseng, G., Poulter, A. and Hiom, D. 3rd edn. London: LA Publishing, 2000. 📖
- **The advanced Internet searcher's handbook**.
  Bradley. P. London: LA Publishing, 1999. 📖
- **A guide to finding quality on the Internet**.
  Cooke, A. London: LA Publishing, 1999. 📖
- **Reference sources on the Internet: off the shelf and on to the web**.
  Diaz, K.D. London: Haworth Press, 1997. 📖
- **The information specialist's guide to searching and researching the Internet and the world wide web**.
  Ackermann, E. and Hartman, K. Chicago: IL Publishing, 1999. 📖
- **Internet research: theory and practice**.
  Fielden, N.L. and Garrido, M. North Carolina: McFarland, Jefferson, 1998. 📖

WHAT IS THE INTERNET?

The Internet is a network of computers that provides links to other computers worldwide. The Internet is a vehicle that transports information (data) from one computer to another. You do not find information *on* the Internet rather you find information *through* using the Internet. Anyone

> **Tip:** *the languages of the Internet and different types of files and applications are many. For more details consult the guides and handbooks cited in this chapter.*

can access the Internet for little or no cost and with very little training. The Internet has many useful elements for the researcher. Figure 10.2 outlines some of the main parts of the Internet which you can use in your search for information and guidance.

If you are to search the Internet effectively and efficiently then you need to know about the different search tools available. Figure 10.3 gives an overview of the main Internet search tools: these are the means to identify and access resources on the Internet. They allow you to do the activities shown in Figure 10.1, including retrieving journal articles and bibliographies, browsing library catalogues, participating in discussion groups and much more.

> **Tip:** *remember that a search of the Internet does not constitute a literature search.*

Anatomy of a URL

Most sites on the Internet have an address. The most common form of address is a URL (Uniform Resource Locator), which gives you the location of the resource on the Internet. Here is an example of a URL (sometimes pronounced *Earl*) address:

http:/niss.ac.uk/link/types/sounds.html

The parts of this are as follows:

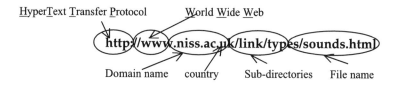

It is important to note the following about URLs:

- URLs contain no spaces, but all the punctuation must be included and done correctly.
- URLs are normally in lower case but if there are some upper-case characters then these must be typed in as such.
- Not all URLs end in a file name. URLs ending with a / will take you to a web page called an Index or similar web page. For example, www.niss.ac.uk/ will take you to the NISS opening page, its index.
- URLs have different domain identifiers, for example:

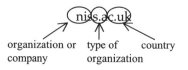

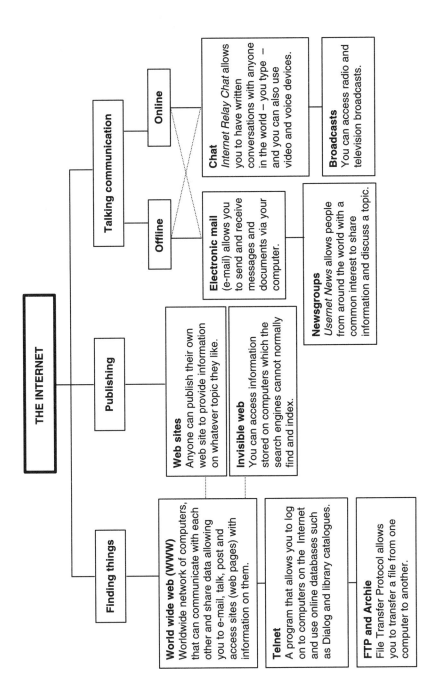

Figure 10.2 *The framework of the Internet*

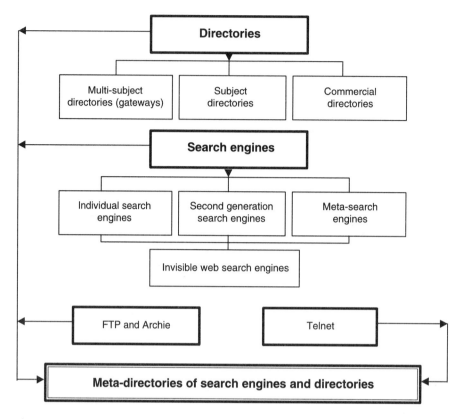

Figure 10.3 *Internet search tools*

The most commonly used address codes for the UK and USA are these:

org	=	trade, industry, charity, voluntary, research association, etc.
com or co	=	commercial, individual, private
ac or edu	=	academic, education
gov	=	government
mil	=	military

- URLs for different types of file have different file extensions and often require an application to be on your computer in order for you to access that type of file. For example, sound files can have, amongst others, the following extensions, **ra, ram** – this means you will need *RealPlayer* (a piece of software) to listen to the sounds on the file. A list of the most common file extensions is given in Appendix 8.

Internet directories

A directory has a series of headings that categorizes resources into subject categories, e.g. business, leisure and culture. There are two basic types of

---

Examples of academic and professional directories (multi-subject gateways) ✿

- **The Argus clearing house**. (www.clearinghouse.net/).
- **BUBL. Link**. (http://bubl.ac.uk/link/).
- **INFOMINE: scholarly Internet resource collection**. (http://infomine.ucr.edu/).
- **Librarian's index to the Internet**. (www.lii.org/).
- **The WWW virtual library**. (www.vlib.org/).
- **Academic info**. (www.academicinfo.net/index.html).
- **The new Athenaeum** (http://members.spree.com/athenaeum/mguide1.htm)
- **Galaxy**. (http://galaxy.com).
- **Scout report signpost**. (www.signpost.org/).
- **Resource discovery network**. (www.rdn.ac.uk/).
- **Galileo: Internet resources**. (www.usg.edu/galileo.html).
- **WebGEMS**. (www.fposol.com/gems/webgems.html).
- **NISS**. (www.niss.ac.uk/).

Examples of subject directories for the social sciences, arts and humanities ✿

- **Research resources for the social sciences.** (www.socsciresearch.com/).
- **Social science research network** (www.ssrn.com/).
- **Resource guide for the social sciences.** (www.jisc.ac.uk/subject/socsci/).
- **Voice of the shuttle.** (http://vos.ucsb.edu/).
- **HUMBUL.** (http://firth.oucs.ox.ac.uk/).
- **SocioSite.** (www.pscw.uva.nl/sociosite/index.html).
- **Social science information gateway.** (www.sosig.ac.uk/).

Examples of university multi-subject directories ✿

- **AlphaSearch.** (www.calvin.edu/library/as/).
- **UCB Internet resources by subject.** (www.lib.berkeley.edu/).
- **Best information on the web** (http://vweb.sau.edu/bestinfo/).
- **TASA Weblinks.** (www.newcastle.edu.au/).
- **CHOICE.** (www.ala.org/acrl/choice.html).
- **OSUL: gateway to information.** (www.lib.ohio-state.edu/gateway/).
- **UHL: Remote access to electronic resources.** (http://info.lib.uh.edu/remote/access.html).
- **University of Albany libraries.** (www.albany.edu/library/internet.html).

Figure 10.3   *Internet search tools (cont.)*

directory (sometimes called portals), *academic and professional directories* and *commercial directories*.

Academic and professional directories   These are usually created and maintained by professional librarians in academic institutions and are therefore generally well organized with the contents vetted for quality and reliability. They often give access to collections and links relevant to research and learning for students, academics and researchers and are normally not-for-profit services though some require a password. Some of these directories are now very large and cover most disciplines taught in universities.

There are two main types of academic directory: *multi-subject directories* which seek and evaluate sources and resources for several disciplines and *subject directories* which focus attention on a particular disciplinary field.

Examples of commercial directories ☆

- **Yahoo**. (www.yahoo.com/).
- **About.com**. (http://home.about.com/).
- **Snap.com**. (www.snap.com/).
- **Magellan**. (http://magellan.excite.com/).
- **Open directory**. (www.dmoz.org/).

Examples of individual search engines (indexes) ☆

AltaVista. (www.altavista.com/).
FastSearch. (www.alltheweb.com/).
HotBot. (http://hotbot.lycos.com/).
Excite. (www.excite.com/).
Lycos. (www.lycos.com/).

Examples of second generation search engines ☆

Google. (www.google.com/).
Northern Light. (www.northernlight.com/).
Direct Hit. (www.directhit.com/).
InferenceFind. (www.infind.com/).
BrightPlanet. (http://brightplanet.com/).
Oingo. (www.oingo.com/).
MetaFind. (www.www.metafind.com/).
Ask Jeeves. (www.askjeeves.com/).
SurfWax. (www.surfwax.com/).

Examples of meta-search engines ☆

Ixquick. (www.ixquick.com/).
Metacrawler. (www.metacrawler.com/).
Inference Find. (www.infind.com/).
Profusion. (www.profusion.com/).
Search.com. (http://search.cnet.com/).
Dogpile. (www.dogpile.com/).
Chubba. (www.chubba.com/).

Figure 10.3   *Internet search tools (cont.)*

Subject gateways collect information on a subject area for a specific user, e.g. psychologists, sociologists or anthropologists. A gateway takes the form of a guide to resources, sources and services from many different information providers and by listing them as *links* gives access to primary and secondary information such as online databases, digitized archives, electronic journals, abstracts and indexes, discussion lists and reference sources such as encyclopaedias.

Information sources and services are selected by academic and professional gateways for their *precision, recall, coverage* and *quality* (and implicitly *relevance*).

- **Precision** refers to how well the retrieved documents match a query.
- **Recall** refers to what fraction of documents are actually retrieved.

- **Coverage** refers to what percentage of relevant documents are indexed by the gateway service.
- **Quality** refers to the scholarly standards of the documents indexed and retrieved.

Contents and links are usually evaluated by subject specialists. A gateway acts as a launch pad to a variety of quality information sources grouped by subject and topic and is a far superior source of information on a topic than a general search engine.

University multi-subject directories   Many universities around the world have multi-subject directories that can be used to find subject-based listings and links to resources and sources. Some, such as those from the Universities of Houston and Berkeley, provide excellent gateways. The University of Kentucky (address – www.uky.edu/Subject/neticsintro.html) also provides a facility for searching the major search engines and many specialist search services using a pro-forma search query form.

Commercial directories   These are services that give access to a range of topics and types of general information on topics such as sport, hobbies, travel and entertainment. They do not usually index academic topics and therefore have few links to research sources and resources. Provided by commercial companies, they rely on advertising to generate income for the service and hence almost anyone can have their web pages indexed on a commercial directory.

Search engines

A search engine is a searchable database of Internet files which have been collected by a computer program. The program collects data by sending out programs known as spiders (also called crawlers, robots, worms, wanderers) on to the Internet to find new and updated web pages. When a new web page is set up it is often *spidered* and automatically added to the database. You use the search engine by typing in your query and the search engine searches its databases and gives you a list of results (hits), often many thousands of pages, matching your query.

There are two main types of search engine, *individual engines* which use spiders to collect for their own databases and *meta-search engines* which search multiple individual engines simultaneously. Meta-search engines do not have their own index, but use the indexes of other search engines to amalgamate the results (often removing duplicates) and present you with a list of pages matching your query.

Second generation search services   Some search engines have been developed to overcome limitations of earlier search engines. These second generation search engines organize results according to concept, site, domain, popularity and linking. Some do this by reading information embedded in the web page that you cannot usually see on the page when it is displayed. Others process your search statement to determine the probable intent of the search.

Some search engines combine the best of first and second generation search engines and some allow the use of *natural language* questions (e.g. 'Who was Karl Marx?') to frame a query (e.g. Ask Jeeves – www. askjeeves.com/ and C4 – www.c4.com/).

Invisible web   Part of the Internet has come to be called the invisible web. This refers to files stored on databases that you can search but which search engines cannot normally spider and therefore do not usually index. If you know the address and file name of a file on the invisible web then you should be able to access it. Addresses are often available from professional associations and other specialist organizations. The following databases do, however, specialize in providing links to databases on the invisible web:

- **Invisible Web.com**
  (address – www.invisibleweb.com/). 🕸
  This provides links to 10,000+ web-accessible databases which would not normally be retrieved by traditional search tools.
- **Direct search page**.
  (address – http://gwis2.circ.gwu.edu/~gprice/direct.htm). 🕸
  Biased towards the USA, this uses broad headings to categorize Internet sources that would not be located by search tools such as Infoseek, HotBot and Alta Vista.

FTP and Archie

File transfer protocol is a program and a method that allows you to access files from one computer and to transfer them to your own computer. Many thousands of computers have databases of files that are generally available for access. These consist of books, articles, reports, data sets and the like. On home computers you can use FTP via the Internet and if you have Microsoft via MS FTP for Windows. Several Internet services can help you to locate FTP files, such as the following:

- **FAST FTP**.
  (address – http://ftpsearch.lycos.com/). 🕸
- **The librarian's guide to the Internet**.
  (address – www.star-host.com/library/). 🕸

If you know the site and the file name then you can type in the address and contact the host computer. If you do not know which site to look at then a basic catalogue of FTP files is available called *Archie*. Archie is a program that searches all the FTP sites on the Internet which are on its list (a crude index). You can access Archie through *The librarian's guide to the Internet* and this gives you access to *Archieplex* (address – www.lerc.nasa.gov/archieplex/doc/form.html), an FTP service provided by NASA (North American Space Agency), that will search for FTP sites and files for you. Other Archie search engines include http://archie.emnet.co.uk/ and www.lights.com/hytelnet/arc000.html. To find other resources on Archie and FTP a general search engine will also be of help.

Telnet

Telnet is a program that allows you to connect and open a link to a remote computer to use online databases, library catalogues and similar resources and sources. To Telnet another computer you need to know its address. This can consist of words and numbers. For JANET, the Joint Academic Network in the UK, the addresses are:

info.ja.net and **192.101.5.160**

The most common electronic-based resources available via Telnet are libraries and databases such as those from *Dialog* (see Chapter 11). For Telnet addresses of the major database providers, hosts and servers see *The library and information professional's guide to the Internet*, Tseng, G., Poulter, A. and Hiom, D. 3rd edn. London: LA, 2000.

FINDING DIRECTORIES AND INTERNET SEARCH ENGINES

There are different ways to identify useful gateways and Internet sources and resources and to keep up to date with developments in specific gateways. Together with the multi-subject directories listed above, consult the following for general lists of directories, search engines and other Internet-related tools, and remember that other chapters in this book give the addresses of other Internet resources for specific topics and subject fields:

- **PINAKEΣ: a subject launch pad.**
  (address – www.hw.ac.uk/libWWW/irn/pinakes/pinakes.html). 🖋
  This provides a listing of the main academic subject and multi-subject gateways and on a regular basis publishes an online newsletter.
- **Librarian's index to the Internet: searching the Internet.**
  (address – www.lii.org/InternetIndex/2/search.html). 🖋
  A set of comprehensive and annotated lists of search engines organized into *best search engines, best subject indexes, meta search engines* and *other search engines.*

- **Beaucoup search engines**.
  (address – www.beaucoup.com/). 🕸
  One of the most complete catalogues of Internet search engines with a directory of more than 1,200 search engines.
- **Search engine guide**.
  (address – www.searchengineguide.com/). 🕸
  Searchable guide to over 2,000 indexes, directories, newsletters and discussion groups.
- **WebRing**.
  (address – www.webring.org/). 🕸
  A directory of web rings, i.e. collections of sites on a similar topic.

Keeping up to date

A number of the multi-subject gateways and other services provide regular updates on developments on the Internet. There are also many print publications but the advantage of Internet sources is their currency. The most efficient and increasingly reliable method to keep a watching brief is to regularly scan sites like the following:

- **Search engine watch**.
  (address – www.searchenginewatch.com/). 🕸
  Comprehensive and well organized lists of search engines with evaluations.
- **Internet resources newsletter**.
  (address – www.hw.ac.uk/libwww/irn/irn.html). 🕸
  A free monthly, non-subscription newsletter for academics and researchers that identifies and evaluates developments on the Internet and new Internet services.
- **Traffick: the guide to portals**.
  (address – www.traffic.com/). 🕸
  Newsletter and descriptions of search engines.
- **Freeprint**.
  (address – www.freeprint.co.uk/). 🕸
  A newsletter with tips and articles on searching the web and useful sites.
- **WhatsNu**.
  (address – www.whatsnu.com/). 🕸
  A weekly alerting service as to what is new on the Internet.

SEARCHING THE INTERNET

The most common problem with a search of the Internet is that you often get thousands (sometimes millions) of results that match your query. This can be avoided if you understand how to search the Internet. Nearly all the multi-subject and subject directories have links to advice on searching the Internet; the following are some which most recommend:

- **UC Berkeley Library**.
  (address – www.lib.berkeley.edu/TeachingLib/Guides/Internet/Find Info.html).
  A comprehensive and regularly updated tutorial on finding information on the Internet.
- **Librarian's index to the Internet: searching the Internet**.
  (address – www.lii.org/InternetIndex/2/search.html).
  An annotated list of links to Internet tutorials and other guides to searching.
- **Freeprint**.
  (address – www.freeprint.co.uk/).
  Tips and articles on searching the web and useful sites.
- **BUBL: Help with searching**.
  (address – http://bubl.ac.uk/searches/guides.html).
  Provides current information and links that give lists of Internet evaluation sites, search engines and advice on searching. Included are **Search engine watch** and **Annotated guide to WWW search engines**.
- **Netskills: network skills for the UK higher education community**.
  (address – www.netskills.ac.uk/).

How to search the Internet

You do not search the Internet by turning on your computer, logging on and typing in whatever term you can think of on your topic. General browsing of available search engines using simple key words and following recommended links is the most effective way to waste your time. Aimless and unplanned browsing is another route to frustration and lack of usable results.

Begin your search with a piece of paper and pen. Analyse your topic and plan how you will do your search, with which search tools. The key to effective and efficient searching is *topic analysis* and *planning*. The following are suggestions on how to analyse a topic and plan a search. For a form that can help you summarize your search see Appendix 9: 'Internet search profile'.

A good place to begin your analysis and plan is in the library using the quick reference section (see Chapter 4), where you can consult guides to the literature and encyclopaedias. This will give you an overview of sources, including Internet web pages and a list of words and phrases for your search vocabulary. An important part of the planning stage is to identify which search tools are likely to be the most relevant for your needs. Table 10.2 in combination with the lists of search engines and directories given above should help you to focus your efforts on relevant search tools. Remember that multi-subject and subject directories are more likely than general search engines to have quality information relevant to your topic.

Table 10.1 *Analysing your topic and planning your Internet search*

What are you looking for?	Before you turn on your computer think about and carefully **analyse your topic** to be certain you know *what* it is you are looking for and why you believe the Internet should be searched.
	If you need to search the Internet then think of words that describe your topic that fit the following list – who/what/where/when/how/why.
What words and phrases describe your topic?	List the distinctive words and phrases that describe your topic,
	e.g. Marx, Marxism, Marxian, Communism, Socialism, Engels, philosopher, economist, historian etc.
	Remember that the word *Marx* will be insufficient because it is too imprecise and will retrieve all persons and things called Marx.
	Has your topic synonymous or equivalent terms which might need to be included,
	e.g. sociologist, Marxist, conflict, structuralism?
	Avoid common verbs, adverbs, adjectives, conjunctions and prepositions, e.g. *a, in, why, it, is,* etc., as these will be ignored by a search engine.
How is your topic classified into levels from general to specific?	Identify the key words for the right level by classifying your search terms into families of terms using who/what/where/when/how/why. Here are some examples for Karl Marx:
	Philosophers = general family of persons and an activity that will give information on *when* Marx lived and *what* he wrote and *who* his contemporaries were. This will give you a general level for searching.
	Marxism = a political philosophy (or ideology) that has many strands. This will give information on *how* Marx's ideas were developed by *who, when* and *why*. This will give you a general level that will possibly give more information than using *Philosophers*.
	Karl Marx = A mid-range-level search that will give biographical and bibliographical information about *who* Marx was and *what* he wrote.
	Das Kapital = This will give you a more detailed level that might provide information on *Das Kapital* (3/4 vols) on *when* and *where* this was published and written and *what* it is about (interpretation). You may also find out *where* to find a copy of the publications and even get a link to digitized versions.
	Karl Marx bibliography = This will take you back to the secondary literature about Marxism but one which is focused on Marx's *Das Kapital* and you will get interpretations of *what Das Kapital* is about, *how* it has been understood, *why* some interpretations are considered better than others, etc. At this level you will get argument and debate about your topic. In practice you will need to look at some of the major secondary works on Marx to find interpretations of his work.

Table 10.1   *(cont.)*

Where do you need to start your search?	Pick the right starting point for your search to save time and effort. This means selecting the right search tools (e.g. search engines and directories) for the level of information that you need. Table 10.2 *Picking the right search tools* will help you to identify which search engines and directories to use.
How can you use symbols to maximize your search terms?	Formulate the words (especially nouns) and phrases into a logical set of search statements identifying what logical operators (i.e. AND, OR etc.) you will use. We talk more about these in Chapter 11.

Table 10.2   *Picking the right search tools*

Think about your needs. Use reference sources before others, e.g. indexes and abstracts.	Use when you have a specific academic topic, want to access OPACs and e-journals, etc.	Use when you have an obscure topic, want particular file types, etc.	For guidance seek help from a professional librarian.

Do you need. . .	Multi-Subject directories	Subject directories	Search engines	Meta-search engines	If in doubt, ask a librarian
Subject directories	✓	✗	✗	✗	✓
Topic overviews	✗	✓	✗	✗	✓
Bibliographies	✓	✓	✗	✗	✓
Biographical information	✓	✓	✗	✓	✓
Electronic journals	✓	✓	✗	✗	✓
Archives	✓	✓	✗	✗	✓
Reference sources	✓	✗	✗	✗	✓
Government information	✓	✗	✗	✓	✓
Statistical information	✓	✓	✓	✗	✓
Discussion groups	✓	✓	✓	✗	✓
Professional contacts	✗	✓	✓	✗	✓
Images	✓	✗	✓	✗	✓

Searching techniques

You can increase the power of your search and thereby maximize the use of your effort and time. The basis of searching technique is the use of basic maths (or math) and Boolean logic. Do not worry about these terms, especially about maths, because all this means is adding to, subtracting from and multiplying your search terms in order to expand (add), narrow (subtract), or include other terms (multiply or combine) to your search. In Chapter 11 we say more about Boolean logic, but the main point to note is that the techniques introduced here can be used with many search engines and with other electronic sources such as CD ROMs and online databases. To get you started we will now look at some initial examples that show how to use search maths and Boolean logic.

WORKED EXAMPLES: INTERNET SEARCHING

The features we will look at are:

1 adding terms to widen your search: the use of **synonyms**;
2 adding symbols to your search to make it more comprehensive: the use of **truncation**;
3 adding terms together to focus your search: the use of the **+ symbol**;
4 subtracting terms to give precision to your search: the use of the **- symbol**;
5 including terms within a search: the use of **parentheses ' '**;
6 combining the above features: doing a **power search**.

1 Synonyms: adds terms to widen the search

A synonym, in computer use, is a word that means the same or nearly the same as another or other words, or the same word used to describe different things:

e.g. *feminine* and *womanly* might be thought to describe similar attributes.
e.g. *Puma* can be used to describe a car, a brand of sports goods and a type of cat, but not any cat.

Use your thesaurus to check for synonyms and your dictionaries for words that have several uses.

Here is an example of a synonym map for **prison** (note that other terms could have been included: reformatory, hulk and clink among others).

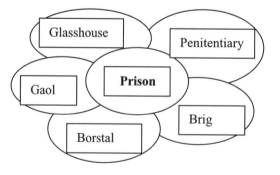

A good list of synonyms will provide wide coverage. Use synonyms to consider whether the inclusion of other terms is also worth using in your search vocabulary and also to decide what terms you want to exclude, e.g. *dungeon(s)* and *brig*.

2 Word stemming: adds terms and widens the search

Some words have the same stem (beginning) and to save time searching for all variations, truncation (or wildcard) can be used to instruct the search to look for all variants based on the stem,

e.g. *Femin*ism, *femin*ist, *femin*ine have the stem *femin*.

To truncate use **?** or ***** symbol, e.g. **femin?** and this will normally retrieve all three (plus other) variants (suffixes) on the stem.
    Remember to use truncation when you want plural *and* singular cases,

e.g. **schools** (plural) in addition to **school** (singular)
e.g. **citations** (plural) in addition to **citation** (singular)

Be careful with truncation. With some truncated words you will retrieve too many variations, e.g. if you use **comm?** you would retrieve many words including communities, community, communism, commute, commutation, etc. The longer the stem, the better truncation works to keep the word number to a minimum.

3 + symbol: adds terms to focus the search

The use of + symbol enables you to add terms together in your search. If you were looking for literature about science fiction (SF) and in particular *Dr Who* and information about the Daleks then you could search this way:

e.g. **+Dr Who +Daleks**

Only the web pages that contain both words would be retrieved. If you further wanted to have information about when Tom Baker, one of a series of actors to play Dr Who, encountered the Daleks then you could add Baker to the search *string*:

e.g. **+Dr Who +Daleks +Baker**

The + enables you to narrow your search when you have been overwhelmed with results ('hits').

4 – symbol: subtracts terms from the search to give precision

The use of the – symbol enables you to find web pages with a particular word on them but not others. If you were looking for other science fiction sites but this time on the original *Star Trek* television series then you might try to exclude all web pages about variations on *Star Trek* such as *Deep space nine*, *Voyager* and the cinema films of Star Trek, e.g. *Star Trek: the motion picture*. This you could do in the following way:

e.g. **star trek -deep -space -nine -voyager -motion -picture**

If you anticipate that a search will retrieve pages with terms you do not want, then use the – symbol to exclude those pages from your results.

5 Phrase searching: multiplies terms for increased precision

The main problem with adding and subtracting terms from your search is the lack of connectivity between the words you use. For example, **+Dr +Who** will retrieve web pages with both words on them but not necessarily in this order or even next to each other. You could therefore retrieve many pages that are irrelevant to your needs. By using phrase searching through the use of quotation marks you can restrict your search to web pages which have *Dr Who* together in sequence, i.e. *Dr* immediately followed by *Who*. To tell the search engine to search for web pages which have *Dr Who* together use quotation marks:

e.g. **'Dr Who'**

You can phrase search with more than two words, e.g. **'Dr Who daleks Baker'** but the more words you use the less likely it is that you will retrieve all web pages about your topic. Try to keep phrase searching sensible and limited to the key words. A much more effective tactic is to combine search maths.

6 Combining search maths

We can now take our examples a little further, to construct very precise searches which have the power to search for what we want and little else. Here are some examples:

To subtract phrases:

e.g. **'star trek' -'deep space nine' -voyager -'motion picture'**

To include nouns in the same web page as a phrase:

e.g. **'Dr Who' +Daleks +Baker**

To look for web pages from a particular country (the UK) and exclude those from other countries:

e.g. **'Dr Who' +host:uk**

To focus on educational sites (*edu* is mainly used in the USA) and exclude others:

e.g. **'jane austen' +host:edu**

To retrieve only government web sites in a particular country:

e.g. **'freedom information' +host:gov.uk**

Most search engines allow the use of the above maths to search. With some (e.g. *Northern Light*) you can use Boolean logic. To find out which engines support Boolean logic consult the sites that give up to date summaries of the search engines such as the University of Berkeley's site (address – www.lib.berkeley.edu/TeachingLib/Guides/Internet/Strategies.html).

Simultaneous searching

Some multi-subject directories provide a facility for the simultaneous searching of several search engines. This saves you time in accessing individual search engines and then searching each one in turn. Examples of *all for one* search services include the following:

- **All4One search machine**.
  (address – www.all4one.com/search_machine.phtml).
- **ProFusion**.
  (address – www.profusion.com/).
- **Search-it-all**.
  (address – www.search-it-all.com/).
- **InfoPeople**.
  (address – www.infopeople.org/src/srctools.html).
- **Webtaxi**.
  (address – www.webtaxi.com/).

SUMMARY OF THIS CHAPTER

- Remember that the Internet is only one among many sources, including print, that should be consulted when conducting a search for literature and data.
- You need to analyse your topic and plan your search before you turn on your computer and remember that there is no universal way to search the Internet.

- The Internet is a self-publishing medium and varies greatly in quality and reliability, so you need to evaluate everything you find.
- Consult sites like *PINAKEΣ: a subject launch pad* to identify academic multi-subject and subject directories.
- The Internet is a rapidly changing environment, therefore keep up to date with new developments.

11

Advanced searching techniques

This chapter will show you:

- how to use online databases such as Dialog and BlaiseLine
- how the online information retrieval industry works
- how to use Boolean logic for searching
- how to do a power search

In order to undertake a successful literature search at doctoral level and for professional research you will need to use online search services such as Dialog. This means that you will need to know about advanced searching techniques. The techniques described in this chapter can also be used with some CD ROM indexes and with some Internet services. For additional advice on the increasing complexity of electronic information and advanced searching see guides such as the following:

- **Information seeking in the online age: principles and practice**.
  Large, J.A. London: Bowker-Saur, 1999.
- **The online searcher's companion**.
  Forrester, W.H. and Rowlands, J.L. London: LA Publishing, 1999.
- **Searching CD ROM and online information sources**.
  Chowdhury, G.G. and Chowdhury, S. London: LA Publishing, 2000.

ONLINE SEARCHING

Carrying out an online search involves accessing a remote computer (site) where the database containing the records you want to search is located. This could mean accessing a database in say California or Switzerland. Most databases can be accessed from home or college using a relatively standard personal computer. The databases are vast stores containing hundreds of thousands of bibliographical records in a range of indexes. These indexes can be used to find relevant materials, e.g. books and articles. Some databases provide the whole document, i.e. an entire article.

These are referred to as full-text databases. With the increased use of telecommunications to access information, more and more databases are becoming full-text.

The main disadvantage of online searching is the cost. Data hosts (or vendors) are able to maintain the database only if searchers pay for their search. An average search can cost around £30 to £50. You have to pay for the telecommunications connection time (i.e. phone) and the time spent searching the database and print costs. There are, however, advantages to online searching. The main one is that a host may have hundreds of separate subject databases on the computer that your library does not have on CD ROM. Some of the databases are general while others are very specific.

Using online hosts, such as Dialog, Datastar and Blaise, is *not* the same as searching the Internet. The cost element alone means that you will need to prepare your search in advance and to do this you must have a sound understanding of the principles of searching. Figure 11.1 gives an overview of the online information retrieval industry.

The easiest way to access an online database is through an academic library. Subject librarians will often help you plan your search. They will also take you through what can sometimes seem complex terms and symbols used by some database hosts. The stages for making the link to the host computer are the same for most databases. Figure 11.1 shows the main elements of the *information link* to data hosts. From a personal computer contact is made to the host computer where the databases are located. Much online searching involves connection to hosts in other countries. You can contact these hosts either through the telephone network or via the nearest *node*, which is an access point that automatically switches the call on to a long distance route. Once connected to the host you can begin to search the databases from services such as those listed below.

Online information retrieval services:

- **BIDS Bath Information and Data Services (UK).**
  (address – www.bids.ac.uk/).
  Provides access to a range of services including ISI citation indexes, UnCover (journal contents) and bibliographic databases.
- **DataStar Web.**
  (address – www.krinfo.ch/krinfo/products/dsweb/).
  Provides databases on health, medicine, law, biotechnology, marketing and business.
- **LEXIS-NEXIS Communication Centre.**
  (address – www.lexis-nexis.com/).
  Provides legal and business reports and news from around the world.
- **OCLC – Online Computer Library Centre.**
  (address – www.oclc.org/).
  OCLC's First Search service provides access to OCLC's online union catalogue of libraries (WebCat) and other well known databases.

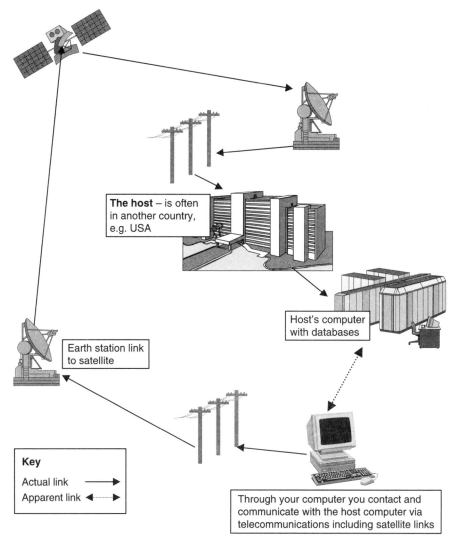

The host – is often in another country, e.g. USA

Host's computer with databases

Earth station link to satellite

Key

Actual link ——▶
Apparent link ◀┄┄▶

Through your computer you contact and communicate with the host computer via telecommunications including satellite links

Figure 11.1   *The framework of the online information retrieval industry*

In addition to the above there are other hosts such as the European Space Agency's Information Retrieval Service (ERA-IRS), Questel-Orbit, Information Access and Ovid Technologies. All of these have databases relevant to the social sciences, arts and humanities but it is Dialog, DataStar and Blaise that have the key databases on the bulk of material you are likely to need.

The elements of the information retrieval industry

The four main elements of the online information retrieval industry shown in Figure 11.1 are the:

1 *database producers*: a combination of commercial, learned societies and organizations and governments. For example, the American Psychological Association produces the main databases for psychology.
2 *databases*: the store of indexes and abstracts in designated subject fields, for example, *Psychological Abstracts*.
3 *hosts* (also referred to as vendors or service suppliers): the commercial organizations that purchase the right to supply the databases from the database producers. They mount the database on their computer and provide access to remote users. They also provide the software to enable the user to search the databases and to order hardcopy reproduction of an article. An example of a major host is Dialog.
4 *telecommunications connections*: the infrastructure that enables users to communicate with the hosts via cheap, long distance telecommunication. The global spread of telecommunications means that most hosts can now be contacted from almost anywhere on the planet.

THE HOSTS

There are many hosts providing access to hundreds of databases. The two we will focus on are Dialog and BlaiseLine.

Dialog   This is one of the largest hosts in the world. It is a general host that does not specialize but offers in excess of 500 different databases along with other services. Although it has a bias towards American publications it gives full access to nearly all the main social science, arts and humanities indexes and abstracts.

Blaise   The British Library Automated Information Service. It has two parts, **BlaiseLink** and **BlaiseLine**. BlaiseLink is a link to the American National Library of Medicine. BlaiseLine provides access to bibliographical databases and catalogues, many of which are not available elsewhere. It also offers access to music, maps, conference proceedings and grey literature through SIGLE.

What the hosts provide

Dialog and BlaiseLine can provide access to nearly all the major and minor bibliographical databases and catalogues needed for an advanced search in the social sciences, arts and humanities.

Dialog (address – http://dialog.krinfo.com/) A small number of the general databases can provide a quick route to key sources. *Social SciSearch* and the *Arts & Humanities Search* available from Dialog, provide in-depth multidisciplinary searching of massive databases. Both *Social SciSearch* and

Arts & Humanities Search allow you to perform 'citation searches' and 'key word searching'.

Citation searching means that if you have the details of an author or a work you can use these to identify current papers which are related to the earlier ones (see Chapter 9 for more details). Key word searching means that the database can be searched by using key words such as an author's name or a word associated with the topic. The databases index all authors and key words from the bibliographical details of the articles they hold. The following summarizes each of these databases.

- **Social Sci Search** (Dialog/ISI)
  Articles from over 1,200 journals covering 22 subject fields are indexed on to the database every week. Relevant articles from a further 3,300 journals in science and technology are also indexed. This amounts to around 100,000 articles added to the database every year. The database extends back to 1972 and currently has around 2.5 million records. The subject areas covered include anthropology, archaeology, communication, criminology, demography, education, linguistics, political science, public health, psychology, sociology and urban studies. You can choose to search a single discipline, several, or across the entire set of databases. You can also limit a search to recent articles or go back to 1972.
- **Arts & Humanities Search** (Dialog/ISI)
  Subject fields covered: articles, letters, editorials, notes, meetings, abstracts, discussions, errata, poems, short stories, excerpts from books, plays, chronologies, bibliographies, music scores and filmographies – over 1,000 arts and humanities journals are indexed every week. Also added to the database are indexes of book reviews, records, films, art exhibitions, television and radio programmes and a selection of journals from social science journals. This amounts to around 100,000 articles per year. The database extends back to 1980 and currently holds around 1.2 million records. Some of the 14 subject areas covered are architecture, art, classics, film, radio and television, folklore, history, literature and philosophy.

Many databases on Dialog are relevant to the social sciences, arts and humanities. Table 11.1 gives an indication of these while Table 11.2 gives an indication of the categories of databases.

BlaiseLine (address – www.bl.uk/services/bsds/nbs/blaise.html) BlaiseLine does not have as many databases (or files) as Dialog but it does have databases that no one else provides. Included among these are the following:

Bibliographic files
  BNB   British National Bibliography 1977—
  HMSO   Her Majesty's Stationery Office 1976—

Table 11.1 *Examples of online databases and database categories from Dialog*

Social sciences and humanities

File name	File number	File name	File number
Academic index	88	Ageline	163
America: history and life	38	Art literature international	191
Arts & humanities search	466	British education index	121
Dissertation abstracts on line	35	Eric	1
Historical abstracts	39	Magill's survey of cinema	299
Mental health abstracts	86	Music literature international	97
Philosopher's index	57	PsycINFO	11
Religion index	190	Social SciSearch	7
Sociological abstracts	37	US political science documents	93

Table 11.2 *Some relevant search categories on Dialog*

Consumer information (Files: 47, 11, 149, 211, 468, 484, 646, 647, 675, 746)
Education (Files: 1, 7, 11, 46, 88, 121)
Foundations and grants (Files: 26, 27, 85)
Language and linguistics (Files: 1, 7, 11, 36)
Library and information science (Files: 1, 2, 6, 61, 202)
Magazines and journals full-text (Files: 122, 442, 624, 646)
People (Files: 47, 88, 234, 236, 287)
Philosophy and religion (Files: 57, 175, 190, 297, 439)
Psychology (Files: 1, 7, 11, 37, 86)
Reference (Files: 287, 137, 470, 77, 35, 480)

ISSN   ISSN Centre for Serials 1965—
LCC   Library of Congress
WHIT   Whitaker 1965—

British Library catalogues
  BLISS   British Library Information Services 1981—
  CONF   British Library Document Supply Centre Conference
           Proceedings 1964—
  DSCM   British Library Document Supply Centre Monographs 1980—
  HSS   Humanities and Social Science 1976—
  SIGLE   System for Information on Grey Literature 1981—
  SSIS   Social Science and Information Service 1974—
  MAPS   Maps 1974—
  MUSIC   Music 1981—

Specialist databases
  ESTC   Eighteenth Century Short Title Catalogue 1701–1800
  ISTC   Incunabula Short Title Catalogue pre-1501
  RPM   Register of Preservation Microforms 1460—

BOOLEAN LOGIC

In order to search online hosts, the Internet and CD ROMS effectively and efficiently, you need to know about the use of Boolean logic. This is the logical system of combining words into a *statement* for searching. You can use Boolean logic to combine search terms in order to frame your search statement. This allows you to specify what you want included in your search and how you want the host computer to search its records. Boolean operators give you the power to narrow your search by enabling you to specify what you are looking for and thereby exclude many irrelevant items. Boolean searching works by using *logical operators* and *specified syntax*. These are combined in Boolean *expressions* (sometimes called *statements*) that the computer uses to search a database. Do not worry about the language, it will all become clear shortly. Table 11.3 gives an overview of Boolean search operators and shows the basic elements and principles of the logic.

It will take you a short time to learn Boolean logic but it will be worth it given the time and effort you will save when searching. Remember that the underlying premise of Boolean logic is set theory: Figure 11.2 shows this in the operator where AND is an intersection operator and OR is a union operator. These are expressed as Venn diagrams which show how the operators work to search for documents matching your instructions.

> **Tip:** *Boolean operators often seem to mean the opposite to what they mean in ordinary language. This is because they do not look like ordinary sentences. Some search services can use ordinary or natural language for searching, e.g. Ask Jeeves.*

Table 11.3 *Boolean terms*

Operator	What it does
AND	Terms on both sides of this operator must be present somewhere in the document in order for it to be identified by the computer as a result (hit), i.e. X AND Y.
OR	Terms on either side of this operator are sufficient to be identified as a result, i.e. X OR Y.
AND NOT	Documents containing the term AFTER this operator are rejected from the results, i.e. X AND NOT Y.
NEAR	Terms only have to be within a specified word distance from one another to be identified as a result, i.e. X NEAR Y (therefore similar to AND).
BEFORE	Only the first term before this operator (within a specified word distance) has to be present for the computer to identify it as a result, i.e. X BEFORE Y.
AFTER	Only the first term AFTER this operator has to be present for the computer to identify it as a result, i.e. X AFTER Y.
Phrases	Combined words that are adjacent to one another for the computer to identify the document as a result, i.e. X Y.
Wildcards	The root of words (sometimes called stem) that the computer must find in order for the document to be identified as a result, e.g. wom? = women and woman (and also completely unrelated words, e.g. wombat).
Parentheses	A way of grouping words or phrases within a statement to exclude others, e.g. 'literature reviewing'.

Logical operator	Search instruction	Venn diagram	Description
AND	Conjunctive intersection	A ( ) B	A × B Both terms A and B must be in a document, e.g. cable × television
OR	Additive union	A ( ) B	A + B Only one of the terms must be in a document for it to be retrieved, e.g. cable or television.
NOT	Subtractive	A ( ) B	A – B One term will be used to search, e.g. fibre optics but not cable.

Figure 11.2   *Boolean maths (adapted from J.E. Rowley, 'Organizing knowledge', Aldershot: Gower, 1988)*

When to use AND and when to use OR

A simple method of deciding when to use AND or OR is to ask, are my key words different concepts or just different ways of saying the same thing? For different concepts use AND and for different synonyms use OR. For example, the words 'fast', 'speed' and 'acceleration' are similar words, therefore you would normally use the OR operator in a search for such words. If you wanted to search for documents with 'acceleration' and 'height' then you would normally use the AND operator. We will now look at the operators in more detail, with some examples.

> **Tip:** *see Chapter 10 for advice on synonyms and word use in searching.*

WORKED EXAMPLES: OPERATORS

AND operator

This instructs your computer to find documents that only contain two specified items. Here is an example that wants to know if pumas are an endangered species.

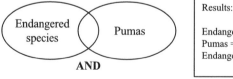

Results:

Endangered species = 145,879
Pumas = 25,602
Endangered species AND Pumas = 4,323

The search has identified documents with both endangered species and pumas. It has not discriminated over *where* in the document the words are located in respect to one another, or if they are linked in any way. Without the AND operator the search might have identified many more documents. 'Puma' is also a model of motor car and sports wear. You can use the AND as a qualifier to focus your search on pumas the animal by using the search phrase **pumas AND cats**. To be more specific and assured you could use a chain of terms, such as **pumas AND 'cats' AND 'endangered species'**. This would only return documents with all three terms in them.

OR operator

This operator instructs your computer to search for documents that contain either word. The OR therefore expands a search. Here is an example.

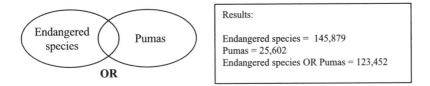

Note that the overall result is not the sum of endangered species + pumas. This is because documents which contain both terms normally get counted as one and search engines make internal evaluations on queries. The result is often less than one of the terms. The OR operator can be used to string words and phrases together using parenthetical clauses, e.g. **London OR 'Westminster' OR 'St Paul's' OR 'Trafalgar'**. Take care when using the OR operator because it can produce far too many results.

AND NOT operator

This operator removes documents that contain a word or phrase that immediately follows the operator. Here is an example.

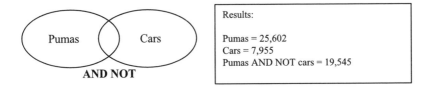

The AND NOT operator will not discriminate between other things called pumas. In this example only the documents with pumas as cars have been eliminated, and then only some of those. This is because some documents about the puma car rather than pumas will not have been eliminated unless a wildcard was used. The AND NOT is an operator that is normally used at later stages in a search to incrementally eradicate irrelevant results.

NEAR operator

The NEAR operator requires that two or more words or phrases are near to one another in a document: this usually means within ten words but you can specify the distance. Here is an example.

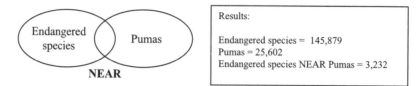

The NEAR operator can be used to ensure that your words appear within the same paragraph. This means that you are more likely to get specific documents on your topic. But you will also be eliminating those documents that discuss pumas in one part and endangered species in another. The NEAR operator is normally used to identify documents that have the terms near to one another.

BEFORE and AFTER operators

These operators work the same way as the NEAR operator but are used to specify which terms or phrases come first or second. The BEFORE operator identifies documents which have the term before the operator and the AFTER identifies documents which have the term AFTER the operator. Few Internet search engines support the use of the BEFORE and AFTER and it is often more effective to use the NEAR.

Parentheses

Most search engines and search services do not read as we normally do, that is from left to right. They read inside-out, that is, they look for words which are included in parentheses. You bound your search terms that are synonyms (e.g. puma, cat) with parentheses (i.e. ' '). A bounded set is called a **Boolean expression**. You can use parentheses with other operators. The main principles are these:

1 Define your expressions with an open and closed parentheses.
2 Try to have your main subject (search concept) first, followed by subsequent terms in order of importance.
3 Make sure you have an equal number of closed and open parentheses in your search query.
4 Expressions at the same level are read in order, from left to right.

Power searching

By thinking carefully about how to search using operators you can do a power search. This means you are maximizing Boolean operators, basic search concepts and syntax to do a combined search. The principle of power searching is to juxtapose three *concepts* in your search query. The first concept should be your subject (the *what*), defined at the proper level, with synonyms or phrases that are appropriate to provide necessary but sufficient coverage of the subject. The other two concepts should correspond to at least two of the following concepts: *when*, *where*, *how* and *why*. For example, who has written what about pumas as an endangered species and on the role of zoos to protect and breed pumas?

> **Tip:** *see Chapter 10 for advice on synonyms, levels and wildcards.*

'puma?' AND 'endangered species' AND 'zoo?'

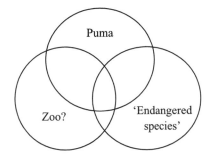

Although you can use more concepts it is advisable to try to limit your concepts to three. This will keep your search sensible and will normally produce relevant results.

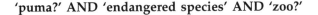

USING ONLINE DATA HOSTS

To search the databases provided by a host you will need to understand how to use *commands*. These are terms and symbols which make up a search language that enables you to provide the relevant instructions to the host computer to search their databases. Different hosts have different command languages; you will need to acquire familiarity with two or three of these. Before we look at the command languages for hosts it is useful to know about the 11 functions that are common to most database searching (including CD ROMs). These are shown in Table 11.4.

The 11 common commands can now be translated into the specific commands for the Dialog and BlaiseLine hosts (Tables 11.5 and 11.6)

There are some obvious things you can do to save time and money when searching online. Assuming there are no other sources you can use apart

Table 11.4 *Eleven common functions in command languages*

Function	Description
1 Logon 'Selecting files' 'Changing file'	There are various ways to make a connection with a host. Each host provides documentation on the procedures for logging on and entering files. Once you have logged on you can select the files (databases) you want to search. You can change files during your session but unless the previous search is saved it will be lost. Type **files** to see a list of the files available. Type **file *filename*** to connect to a different file, e.g. **file lc** to connect to the current *Library of Congress* database.
2 Select search terms 'Qualifiers'	Simply enter your search terms and instruct the host to search the file you have selected. With Dialog a command is needed to enter search terms. To narrow your search you can add qualifiers such as year of publication.
3 Combining search terms 'Logical operators'	If you need to use more than one search term then you can combine terms by using what are called *logical operators* – **and, or, not** – e.g. dogs **and** cats. Each host has a different way of using logical operators.
4 Truncation 'Embedded truncation'	Truncation is a device you can use to avoid typing several separate words which all start with the same root, e.g. computing and computer start with *comput* (the root). If you type in **comput?** in Dialog you will retrieve *computing, computers, computerization*. Some words have alternative spelling in the middle, e.g. woman and women. All variations of such words can be retrieved using embedded truncation, e.g. **wom?n**.
5 Field qualifiers	You can instruct the computer to limit your search to a particular element of the field, e.g. the title or the abstract. If you specify search only for a term in the title then all other elements of a field (record) will be ignored.
6 Proximity operators	These allow you to enter a short phrase and instruct the computer to look for those words in proximity to each other, e.g. **literature(W) review(W)breast(W)cancer**. This is instructing the computer to search for articles which have these terms next to each other in this order. You can be more specific by using an **S**: this asks the computer to search for terms in the same sentence.
7 Direct limits	Once you have some hits then you might want to narrow the search by instructing the computer to retrieve only those records which meet a particular criterion, e.g. English language only.
8 Dictionary files	Some hosts give you access to what are called dictionary files. These enable you to look at your search terms and to see if there are any variations, say, in an author's name or initials, e.g. Radway, J. and Radway, J.A, might both be the same author.

Table 11.4   *(cont.)*

Function	Description
9 Display	You need to see the records which the computer has retrieved for you and you do this by selecting **display**. The displayed records are often called online prints. Remember that each document you display adds to the final cost of your search.
10 Printouts	Different hosts allow different levels of direct printing of the records retrieved. In some cases you have to request the host to print out and send you your records while others allow you to print out your records – but all charge you for the service.
11 Logging-off	You disconnect from the host by logging-off. Before you log-off the cost of your search will be displayed on the screen.

Table 11.5   *Dialog: command language*

Select your files	Once you have logged-on to Dialog you can select the files you want to search. At the prompt: ?BEGIN enter the number of the file(s) you want to search, e.g. **?SET FILES ALL**. This will search about 390 files (separate databases). To be more specific, type in the number of the file you want to search, e.g. **?N7** (*Social SciSearch*).
Select your search terms	S = a term SS = two or more terms e.g. **?ss Alzheimer? AND Drug?**
Results	The system will then respond with your results: ?SET FILES HITS You have 159 files
Refine and narrow your search	You might want to narrow your search by adding more terms and restrictions, e.g. **?S Alzheimer? AND Drug? AND clinical (W) trial?** Note the truncation of terms using **?**
Search the dictionary and help files	You can see what other words can be used to search for Alzheimer's by using the Dictionary Files, e.g. ? expand search term ? e Alzheimer? You will be shown an alphabetical list of 12 terms from the basic index or specific index. Your term will be marked with an asterix *. To get help with your search use the help command ? **EXPLAIN**, e.g. ? **EXPLAIN format**.
Combining search terms	To combine search terms use the logical operators **AND, OR** and **AND NOT**. **AND** links terms in the following way: e.g. **?S Alzheimer? AND Drug? AND clinical (W) trial?**

Table 11.5   *(cont.)*

Proximity searching	To search for words that appear next or near to each other use the following commands: **(w)** or **0** requires words to be adjacent and in the specified sequence; **(n)** only requires words to be adjacent. Use a number e.g. **(3n)** to specify the degree of adjacency, i.e. 3 words may be between the specified term(s).
Limit the search	You can limit your search by using field qualifiers. To do this use a series of two-letter codes which are specified in Dialog's guides to searching. For example, to also specify that one or more of your search terms be present in the title of an article, use **ti**, and that it be published in a particular year, use **py=** followed by the year: e.g. **py=1999** would select documents published in 1999.
Displaying, downloading and printing results	You can *display* your results by using **? d** command. For example, **? d S1-5** will display results 1 to 5. You can define the format for how your chosen records can be displayed (brief or expanded formats) by selecting from pre-defined formats and if you have more than one set of records you can choose which one to display, e.g. **? d/S(number)**/format number/range of records, i.e. **? d S1/3/1-5**, displays records 1–5 from set one, in format three. To see all your records retrieved in rank order use **? RANK FILES**. This ranks the files in order of the most hits. You can *download* results into a word-processing package. To do this open a document file (e.g. Word) on a floppy disk in the A drive, give the file a name, create a shortcut to the A drive, from Dialog with your results displayed, use select all and copy, and toggle back to the Word file, and paste. Your results including the data on your search will be pasted into a Word document for you to use. If you need to *print* off all the records retrieved use **T** or **type** instead of **d** and **display**.
Logging-off	Log-off and finish your session using **LOGOFF**.

Source: adapted from *Dialog search feature*, Miller, C. Palo Alto, California: Dialog Corp, 1993

Table 11.6 *BlaiseLine: command language*

Select your files	Once you have logged-on to BlaiseLine you can select the files you want to search.
	Type in: *file filename*, e.g. **file lc**.
	Help is available by typing in: *explain filename*, e.g. **explain lc**.
Enter your search terms	Enter your search term (word or phrase) after the USER cue that looks like this:
	USER 1?
	USER: (the system prompts you for your first search term), e.g. **cats**
Results	The system will then respond with your result:
	PROG:
	SEARCH 1 FOUND 200 ITEMS
	The system found 200 items using an unqualified search in all fields of the records, i.e. title, series, abstract, author, etc.
Qualifiers	You might want to narrow your search by adding qualifiers, e.g. search for cats only in the title.
	SEARCH 2? Useful search qualifiers are, tw=title, au=author,
	USER: cats (tw) pu=publisher, yr=year of publication.
	PROG:
	SEARCH 3 FOUND 78 ITEMS.
Search the dictionary	You can see what other words can be used to search for cats by using the NEIGHBOUR or NBR command to take you to an alphabetical list.
	nbr history You can move up and down the list and select
	Or from it which items you want to look at or
	nbr history (tw) search.
	This will give you a list like this:
	Cato n(au)
	Catoire (tw)
	Cats (pd)
	Cats (tw)
Truncating terms	To truncate a term you put a colon (**:**) or # after the stem, e.g.
	SEARCH 3?
	USER:
	Pollut#: *finds pollution, pollutant, etc.*
	Horse# *finds horse, horses, etc.* You can use: or # in the middle of a term, e.g. woman and women as wom#n.

Table 11.6   *(cont.)*

Combining search terms	To combine search terms use the logical operators **AND**, **OR** and **AND NOT**. **AND** links terms in the following way, SEARCH 1? USER: Cats AND dogs This will look for records with the terms cats and dogs in the field. **OR** instructs the computer to look for either or any of the terms. **AND NOT** instructs the computer to look for records that contain the first term but not the second.
Proximity searching	To search for words that appear next to each other use the command **ADJ** or **@** or **NEAR** e.g. mass ADJ media This will request that words adjacent to one another are searched for example, balloons NEAR airships, will search for the words in the same record in any order.
Direct limits	You can limit your search by using field qualifiers. A list of qualifiers is available from BlaiseLine. This is the same as qualifying your search using the following kind of code, (PL)=publication place, e.g. Milton Keynes (YR)=year e.g. 1998 (AM)=conference name as author
Displaying and printing results	You can display your results by using **PRT BR** command. This will give you the title of a work and will print out all the records from your last search. Use the following for more detailed printouts, **PRT FU** for the full print format and **PRT DL** for the full record.
Logging-off	Log-off and finish your session using **Stop Y**.

from online databases, the key thing is to plan the search using the following questions as guides:

- What is the main topic?
- Which concepts describe the topic?
- What are the relationships between the concepts?
- How should the concepts be ranked in order of importance?
- What terms and synonyms can be used?
- Have you a key author or paper that can be used to do citation searching?
- What limits can you place on the search, e.g. languages, dates, etc.?
- Have you read the instructions and guides for searching online databases?

- Which databases do you need to search?
- Have you written down your search plan?

Using your answers to the above questions and the preparation you did for other aspects of your search you should be able to search an online host.

SUMMARY OF THIS CHAPTER

- Online hosts often give access to most of the major indexing and abstracting services along with many specialized services for a fee.
- There are several online hosts. The main ones relevant to the social sciences, arts and humanities are Dialog, BlaiseLine and DataStar, which can be accessed through an academic library and the Internet.
- Some of the most useful databases are Social SciSearch and Arts & Humanities Search (from Dialog) and BNB (from BlaiseLine).
- Pre-search planning is the key to an efficient and effective use of online hosts.

Appendix 1: the Dewey Decimal Classification and Library of Congress Classification

DEWEY DECIMAL CLASSIFICATION (DDC)

000 Generalities
Includes: reference, computing, the Internet, library and information science, museums, news, publishing.

100 Philosophy and psychology
Includes: ethics, paranormal phenomena.

200 Religion
Includes: bibles, religions of the world.

300 Social sciences
Includes: sociology, anthropology, statistics, politics, economics, law, government, public administration, social services, education, commerce, communications, standards, customs.

400 Language
Includes: linguistics, language learning, specific languages.

500 Natural sciences and mathematics
Includes: general science, mathematics, astronomy, physics, chemistry, earth sciences, palaeontology, biology, genetics, botany, zoology.

600 Technology (applied sciences)
Includes: medicine, psychiatry, applied physics, engineering, agriculture, home economics, management, accounting, chemical engineering, food technology, metallurgy, manufacturing.

700 The arts
Includes: art, planning, architecture, photography, music, games, sport.

800 Literature and rhetoric
Includes: literature of specific languages.

900 Geography and history
Includes: geography and history of the ancient and modern world, archaeology.

LIBRARY OF CONGRESS CLASSIFICATION (LCC)

A	General works
B	Philosophy and religion
C–F	History
G	Geography
H	Social sciences
J	Political science
K	Law
L	Education
M	Music
N	Fine arts
P	Literature
Q	Science
R	Medicine
S	Agriculture
T	Technology
U	Military science
V	Naval science
Z	Bibliography and library science

Subdivisions: H Social science

H	School science: general works
HA	Statistics
HB–HJ	Economics
HM	Sociology: general works
HN	Social history, social problems, social reform
HQ–HT	Social groups
HV	Social pathology, public welfare, criminology
HX	Socialism, communism, anarchism

Appendix 2: Dewey Decimal Classes for sample subjects

Sociology		Government		Economics	
Community action	361.6	Administrative law	342.410	Austrian economics	330.15
Deviance: sociology	302.5	Central government	354	Banking	332.1
Economics	330	Colonialism	325.3	Development economics	330.91
Ethnic groups:		Communism		Econometrics	330.01
Health & welfare	362.84	Economics	335.43	Economic geography	330.91
Education	370.19	Political ideologies	320.532	Economics	330
Sociology	305.8	Comparative government	320.3	European economics	330.94
Gender identity	305.3	Constitutional law	342.41	European economies	337.14
Industrial sociology	306.36	Economics	330	Financial accounting	657.48
Labour economics	331	Education	370	Financial economics	332
Marriage & family	306.8	State education	379	Financial management	658.15
Mass media: sociology	302.23	Elections	324.6	History of economic thought	330.09
Methodology: sociology	301.01	Internal law	341	Industrial economics	338
Philosophy	180–19	International relations	327	Industrial relations	331
Politics	320	Law enforcement	363.2	Inflation	332.41
Pressure groups	322.43	Legislation	328	Internal economics	337
Psychology	150	Local government	352	International finance	332.04
Religion	200	Parliament: legislation	328.41	Investment	332.6
Religion: sociology of	306.6	Police powers	345.42	Keynesian theory	330.15
Social anthropology	306	Police services	363.2	Labour economics	331
Social change	303.4	Political parties	324.2	Law	340
Social classes	305.5	Political theory	320.01	Macroeconomics	339
Social conflict	303.6	Politics	320	Marxian economics	335.4
Social control	303.33	Practical politics	324.7	Mathematics	510
Social history	940–99	Pressure groups	322.43	Microecomomics	338.5
Social policy	361.61	Psychology	150	Monetary policy	332.46
Social psychology	302	Public administration	350	Operations research	001.42
Social work	360	Social policy	361.61	Politics	320
Sociological research	301.07	Socialism: economics	335	Privatization	354.41
Sociological theory	301.01	Sociology	301	Public finance	336
Urban renewal	711.4	Statistics	310	Public sector economics	336.41
Urban sociology	307.76			Statistics	519.5
Women: sociology of	305.4			Taxation	336.2
Women: welfare	362.83			UK economy	330.94
				Unemployment	331.13
				Welfare economics	330.15

English Literature		Media and Communication		Social Work	
Anglo-saxon	429	Advertising: copywriting	659.132	Adoption	362.7
Applied linguistics		Broadcasting: radio	384.54	Child abuse	362.70
General	418	TV	384.55	Child placement	362.73
English	428	Cinema: production	791.43	Child protection	362.71
Bibliographies: language	016.4	sociology	302.234	Children's act	344.41
Bilingualism	404.2	Communication: (302.5)	001.51	Criminology	364
Computing	004–00	sociology	302.2	Custodianship	346.42
Computing & literature	802.85	Culture: history (901.9)	909	Diseases	616
Dialectology	417	sociology	306	Elderly: home care	649.8
Dialects: English	427	English language	420	medicine	618.97
Dictionaries: general	403	History: Europe	940	psychology	155.67
English language	423	Journalism: news media	070.1	social problems/services	362.6
English language	420	reporting	070.43	Ethnic minorities	362.84
Etymology: general	412	Keyboarding	652.3	Foster care	362.73
English	422	Mass media	302.23	Housing	363.5
Grammar: general	415	Newspapers: history	072.1	Law: criminal	345
English	425	Newspaper industry:		family	346.41
History of English language	420.9	economics	338.470	Medicine	610
Language: general	400	Newspapers: journalism	070.172	Mental illness	
English	420	mass media	392.232	social problems/services	362.2
Language learning: education	372.6	Office automation	651.8	Mental retardation	
Lexicography	413.02	Photography:		social problems/services	362.3
Linguistics	410	film/TV	778.5	Physical handicaps	
Non-standard English	427	Photo-journalism	778.99	social problems/services	362.4
Notations/alphabets	411	Politics	320	Physical illness	
Philosophy of language	410	Press freedom	323.445	social problems/services	362.1
Phonology: general	414	Press law	343.420	Poverty	362.5
English	421.5	Professional ethics:	174.90	Prison	365
Reading: applied linguistics	428.4	journalism		Probation	364.63
education	372.4	Propaganda	303.37	Psychiatry	616.89
Semantics: general	412	Public relations	659.2	Psychology	150
English	422	Radio: broadcasting	384.54	Social policy	361.61
Semiotics	001.56	production	791.44	Social security	368.4
Sociolinguistics	401.9	Shorthand	653.424	Social welfare	361
Speech disorders	616.85	Sociolinguistics (306.44)	401.9	Social work theory	361.1
Translation/interpretation	418.02	Sociology	301–307	Sociology	301
Usage: general	418	Television: broadcasting	384.55	Statistics	310
English	428	production	791.45	Therapists	616.89
Voice and speech	612.78	Video production	791.43	psychology	155.4
		Writing: creative	808.042	social problems	362.7
		professional	808.066		

Appendix 3: literature search profile

Topic:

Limits
Dates:
Language(s):
Country:
Exclude:

Key words

Notes

Appendix 4: how to cite sources

WHAT IS REFERENCING (CITING)?

Referencing (or citing) is the systematic recording of all relevant details of a work that you use in your own writing. References can be works cited in the text of your dissertation or thesis, often placed at the end of each chapter, to acknowledge attribution, or if not referred to in the text, placed in a general bibliography at the end of the dissertation or thesis.

WHAT SHOULD YOU REFERENCE?

You should reference all information that you intend to use in your research and this includes unpublished work, such as theses, as well as published work and materials found on the Internet. When searching for relevant literature, record the full bibliographical details of everything you believe might be useful to your own research.

HOW DO YOU REFERENCE THE WORK OF OTHERS?

There is no universal way to reference the work of others. Different subject disciplines have differing ways of referencing work and with the increasing diversity in publications caused by the Internet there are now many different sources to reference. The following suggestions for referencing have been compiled from the following sources and from publishers' guides (e.g. Sage Publications):

- **Modern Language Association.**
  http://cctc.commnet.edu/mla/practical_guide.htm
- **University of Texas at Austin, undergraduate writing center.**
  www.utexs.edu/depts/uwc/.html/citation.html
- **University of Sheffield Library (UK).**
  www.shef.ac.uk/~lib/libdocs/hsl-dvc2.html
- **International Standards Organization ISO 690–2: information and documentation – bibliographic references.**
  www.nlc-bnc.ca/iso/tc46sc9/standard/690-2ehtm
- **Bedford/St Martin's: citation styles.**
  www.bedfordstmartins.com/online/citex.html

The key points to remember when writing references for your bibliographies are:

1 **Keep them clear**: separate your references so your reader can see where one begins and another one ends.
2 **Keep them consistent**: reference similar materials in the same way.
3 **Keep them correct**: give all necessary information.

CITING PRINT SOURCES

Books

Textbooks and monographs

Citation order:

Author surname, initial(s) (if more than one, cite all authors)
Year of publication
Title (italicized)
Place of publication
Publisher

Example: Hart, C. (1998) *Doing a literature review: releasing the social science research imagination.* London: Sage.

Edited books

Citation order:

Editor(s) surname(s), initial(s) (ed.)
Year of publication
Title (italicized)
Place of publication
Publisher

Example: Darling, C. (ed.) (1998) *Collected works of Ronald E. Pepin*. New Haven, CT: Yale University Press.

Translation

Citation order:

Original author, surname, full first name(s)
Year of publication
Title (italicized)
trans. Translator's full name
Place of publication
Publisher

Example: Borges, Jorge Luis (1962) *Ficciones,* trans. Anthony Kerrigan. New York: Grove Press.

Chapter, essay or article in a collection or anthology

Citation order:

Author(s), surname(s), initial(s)
Year of publication
Title of the chapter (quotation marks ' ') in
Title of publication (italicized)
ed. or (eds) Editor(s) name
Place of publication
Publisher

Example: Francis, D. and Hart, C. (1997) 'Narrative intelligibility and membership categorization in a television commercial', in *Culture in action: studies in membership categorization and analysis*, ed. Hester, S. and Eglin, P. Washington, DC: University Press of America.

Articles

Citation order:

Author(s), surname(s), initial(s)
Year of publication
Title (quotation marks ' ')
Journal title (italicized)
Volume, part (in brackets)
Pages (pp)

Example: Hart, C., Shoolbred, M., Butcher. D. and Kane, D. (1999) 'The bibliographic structure of fan information', *Collection Building*, 18 (2): 81–90.

Reference material (dictionaries, encyclopaedias, serials, bibliographies and indexes)

Dictionaries and encyclopaedias

Citation order:

Title (italicized)
Edition
Editor(s)
Volume, part (in brackets)
Publisher
Year of publication

Examples: *New encyclopaedia Britannica*, 15th edn, 32 vols. Encyclopaedia Britannica, 1986; *Chambers twentieth century dictionary*, ed. Macdonald, A.M. Chambers, 1972.

Encyclopaedia article

Citation order:

Author(s), surname(s), initial(s)
Year of publication
Title (quotation marks ' ') in
Title of encyclopaedia (italicized)
Editor(s)
Volume, part (in brackets)
Place of publication
Publisher
Pages (pp)

Example: Halfpenny, P. (1993) 'Explanation', in *The Blackwell dictionary of twentieth century social thought*, ed. Outhewaite, W. and Bottomore, T. Oxford: Blackwell, pp 217–218.

Conferences

Full conference proceedings

Citation order:

Editor (ed.)
Year of publication
Title of conference proceedings: subtitle (italicized)

Location and date of conference
Publisher

Example: Martensson, N. (ed.) (1984) *Industrial robot technology: proceedings of the 7th International Conference on Industrial Robot Technology*, Gothenburg, 2–4 October IFS, 1984.

Conference papers

Citation order:

Author of paper
Year of publication
Title of paper (quotation marks ' ')
Presented at, conference organizers, title of conference: subtitle (italicized)
Location and date of conference

Example: Hart, C. (1994) '"By gum pet you smell gorgeous": representations of sexuality in perfume advertisements'. Presented at, *British Sociological Association Annual Conference, Sexualities in Social Context*, University of Central Lancashire, 28–31 March.

Parliamentary and official publications

House of Commons and House of Lords Papers

Citation order:

GREAT BRITAIN. Parliament. House of. . .
Title (italicized)
Session, year (s)
Publisher, year of publication
Paper number (in brackets)

Examples: GREAT BRITAIN. Parliament, House of Commons, *Safety in outdoor activity centres: second report from the Education Committee*, Session 1994–95. HMSO, 1995 (HC 1994–95 178); GREAT BRITAIN. Parliament. House of Lords, *Europol: tenth report from the Select Committee on the European Communities*, Session 1994–95. HMSO, 1995 (HL 1994–95 51).

Bills (either House of Commons or House of Lords)

Citation order:

GREAT BRITAIN. Parliament. House of . . .
Title (italicized)
Publisher, year of publication
Bill number (in brackets)

Example: GREAT BRITAIN. Parliament. House of Commons, *Home Rule (Scotland) Bill*. HMSO, 1995 (Bills 1994–95 34).

Acts of Parliament

Citation order:

Title (italicized)
Name of Act: Elizabeth II. Chapter no. (italicized)
Publisher, year of publication

Example: *Criminal Justice and Public Order Act 1994: Elizabeth II. 1994. Chapter 33.* HMSO, 1994.

Command papers

Citation order:

GREAT BRITAIN. Name of Committee or Royal Commission
Title (italicized)
Chairperson (if one)
Publisher, year of publication
Paper number (in brackets, Cmnd for Command)

Example: GREAT BRITAIN. Committee on Standards in Public Life, *Standards in public life: the first report of the Committee on Standards in Public Life.* Chairman Lord Nolan. HMSO, 1995 (Cmnd 2850–I & II).

Non-parliamentary or departmental publications

Citation order:

GREAT BRITAIN. Name of Government Department
Title (italicized)
Publisher, year of publication
Series (in brackets)

Example: GREAT BRITAIN. Department of the Environment, *Landfilling wastes.* HMSO, 1986 (Waste Management paper: 26).

EC (EU) publications

Citation order:

EUROPEAN COMMUNITIES. Name of EC Institution.
Title (italicized)
Place of publication, publisher, year of publication
Series (in brackets)

Example: EUROPEAN COMMUNITIES. Commission, *Waste management planning in the European Community.* Luxembourg: Office for Official Publications of the European Communities, 1994 (Document).

Dissertations and theses

Citation order:

Author (surname followed by initials)
Year of publication
Title of thesis
Degree statement (PhD)
Degree-awarding university/body
Supervisor (for MA/MSc) (Sup:), Director of Studies (for PhD) (DoR:) and their institution (in brackets)

Example: Hart, C. (1993) 'The social production of an advertisement'. PhD thesis, Manchester Metropolitan University/J.Walter Thompson Ltd. DoRs: Dr D.W. Francis (Manchester Metropolitan University) and Dr W.W. Sharrock (Victoria University of Manchester).

Newspaper, magazines and periodical articles

Citation order:

Author (surname followed by initials)
Date (year)
Title (quotation marks ' ')
Publication title (italicized)
Place of publication (in brackets)
Day, month and page number(s) (p. or pp)

Example: Norman, M. (1990) 'The once-simple folk tale analyzed by academe', *The Independent* (London), 8 February, p. 15.

Reviews

Citation order:

Name of the reviewer, surname, initials (if indicated)
Date (in brackets)
Title of the review (quotation marks ' ')
Review of . . .
Title of reviewed work (italicized)
Author(s) of reviewed work, full name
Journal information (journal title underlined)
Date and page(s)

Example: Lardner, S. (1980) 'Third eye open'. Review of *The Salt Eaters*, by Toni Cade Bambara. New Yorker, 5 May, p. 169.

Pamphlets and brochures

Citation order:

Title of publication (quotation marks ' ')
Organization/sponsor (italicized)
Place of publication
Publisher
Year of publication

Example: 'Colleges: good for Connecticut, good for you!' *State-wide Council on Saving Connecticut for Community Colleges*. Hartford: Capital Press, 1997.

VISUAL AND AUDIO-VISUAL MATERIAL

Citation order:

Author (surname, initials) or programme name (italicized)
Year of publication/broadcast
Title of production
Medium [square brackets]
Place of publication, organization
Other details, if any

Examples: Peters, T. (1991) *Tom Peters Live* [Audiocassette]. Boulder, CO: CareerTrack Publications; *Pride and Prejudice* (1997) [Video]. London: BBC; Henderson, David (1985) *Reith Lectures*. BBC Radio 3 and 4. November–December.

Individual items within a programme should be cited as contributions:

Example: Thatcher, Margaret (1986) 'Interview', in *Six O'Clock News* [TV], BBC 1. 29 January, 18.00hrs.

CITING ELECTRONIC SOURCES

CD-ROM

Citing an entire CD-ROM bibliographical database

Citation order:

Database (as is on CD ROM)
[CD-ROM]
Inclusive dates (in round brackets)
Place, producer
Available
Distributor file (if any)

Example: AGRICOLA [CD-ROM]. (1970–1978) Beltsville: National Agricultural Library (Producer). Available: SilverPlatter.

Abstract/Index entry to give information sufficient for retrieval of the abstract/index entry from the database Example: Green, P.S. (1989) 'Fashion colonialism: French export "Marie Claire" makes in-roads' [CD-ROM]. *Advertising Age*, 23 October. Abstract from: ABI/INFORM Item: 89–41770.

Citing a journal/newspaper article from a full-text CD-ROM database

Citation order:

Author surname, initials
Year of publication
Title of article (quotation marks ' ')
Journal/newspaper title (italicized)
[CD-ROM]
Volume, date (day, month), page(s)

Example: Lascelles, D. (1995) 'Oil's troubled waters', *Financial Times* [CD-ROM], 11 January 1995, p. 18.

Online databases

Citing an entire online bibliographical database Citation order: same as for citing an entire CD-ROM bibliographical database except there may be no date.
    Example: ABI/INFORM [online]. Louisville: UMI/Data Courier (Producer). Available: DIALOG File: ABI/INFORM (15).

Citing a journal abstract/index entry from an online bibliographical database Citation order: same as for citing a journal abstract/index entry from a CD-ROM database.
    Example: Barmash, I. (1989) 'Talking deals: Dillard's desire for Vendex Stake' [Online], *New York Times*, 2 February 1989. Abstract from: DIALOG File: Courier Plus (484) Item: 00002042.

Citing a full text item from an Online bibliographical database

Citation order:

Author surname, initial(s)
Year of publication

Title of article (quotation marks ' ')
Journal title (italicized).
Volume (part), pages.
Full-text [online]. Online database name (as given on database)
Host [accessed date].

Example: Newens, A.J. et al. (1997) 'Changes in reported dietary habit and exercise levels after an uncomplicated first myocardial infarction in middle-aged men', *Journal of Clinical Nursing*, 6 (2): 153–160. Full-text [online]. CINAHL, Ovid Technologies Inc. [accessed 28 May 1998].

Citing electronic journals

Citation order:

Author surname, initials
Year of publication
Title of article (quotation marks ' ')
Journal title (italicized) [online], volume (part),
Location within the host
Available from: URL [accessed date].

Example: Bradshaw, A. (1998) 'Charting some challenges in the art and science of nursing', *Lancet* [online], 351 (9100): 438–440. Available from: http://www.thelancet.com/newlancet/sub/issues/vol351no9100/essay438.html [accessed 24 March 1998].
   Example of articles from journals only available online: Brown, M.A. (1996) 'Primary care nurse practitioners: do not blend the colors in the rainbow of advanced practice nursing', *Online Journal of Issues in Nursing* [online], 1 August 1996. Available from: http://www.nursingworld/ojin/tpc1/tpc1_6.htm [accessed 17 March 1998].

FTP

Citation order:

Author or file
Date (the one included with the source in round brackets)
Title (quotation marks ' ')
[Online]
Complete telnet address, along with directions to access the publication
Available FTP: Directory: File: date accessed [in square brackets].

Example: King, M.L. (August 1963) 'I have a dream' [online]. Available FTP: mrcnext.cso.uiuc.edu Directory: gutenberg/freenet File: i-have-a-dream: [accessed 2 March 1998].

TELNET

Citation order:

Author (if known), surname, initial(s)
Date (in round brackets give 'no date' statement if the date of publication is not given in the source)
Title (quotation marks ' ')
[online]
Complete telnet address, along with directions to access the publication.
Available Telnet: Directory: File: Date accessed [in square brackets]

Example: Perot, R. (1992) 'An America in danger' [online]. Available Telnet: gopher.tc.umn .edu Directory: Libraries/Electronic Books File: An America in Danger: [accessed 14 June 1998].

Book published online

Citation order:

Author(s) surname, initial(s) (all authors)
Year of publication (original)
Title (italicized)
Complete address, along with directions to access the publication.
Date accessed [in square brackets].

Examples: Du Bois, W.E.B. (1903) *The souls of black folk*. Chicago. Project ed. Steven van Leeuwen. December 1995. Columbia University. www.cc.columbia.edu/acis/bartleby/ dubois/ [accessed 2 December 1997]; Harnack, A. and E. Kleppinger (2000) 'Preface. Online! A reference guide to using Internet sources'. Boston: Bedford/St Martin's, 5 January, http:// www.bedfordstmartins.com/online/ [accessed 19 April 2000].

Electronic conferences (interest groups) and bulletin boards

Citing a message

Citation order:

Author of message
Date of message (in round brackets)
Subject of the message (quotation marks ' ')
Electronic conference or bulletin board (italicize)
[online]
Available e-mail: e-mail address
Date accessed [in square brackets].

Example: Peters, W.R. (11 August 1995) 'International finance questions', *Business Libraries Discussion List* [online]. Available e-mail: BUSLIB-L@IDBSU.BITNET [accessed 11 August 1995].

Professional site

Citation order:

Author/title
Site name (italicize)
Date posted
URL: http: // Internet address /remote path
Date accessed [in square brackets].

Example: Mortimer, Gail, *The William Faulkner Society Home Page*, 16 September 1999. William Faulkner Soc. 1 Oct. 1999 http://www.utep.edu/mortimer/faulkner/mainfaulkner.htm. [accessed 17 April 2000].

Scholarly project or information database

Citation order:

Name of project/database (italicize)
Editors

Date posted
Organization
URL: http: // Internet address /remote path
Date accessed [in square brackets].

Example: *Center for Reformation and Renaissance Studies,* eds. Laura E. Hunt and William Barek. 11 May 1998. U of Toronto. http://CITD.SCAR.UTORONTO.CA/crrs/index.html. [accessed 18 April 2000].

Citing individual works/pages – World Wide Web

Citation order:

Title of site/publication (italicize)
Title of article (quotation marks ' ')
URL: http: // Internet address /remote path
Date accessed [in square brackets].

Examples: *PC Magazine,* 'This month', URL: http://www.zdnet.co.uk/mags/pcmag/thismonth_pcmag.html. [accessed 14 August 1998]; 'Student grants and loans: a brief guide for higher education students'. URL: http://www.open.gov.uk/dfee/loans/loans.htm. [accessed 30 September 1998].

Appendix 5: examples of subject dictionaries

Anthropology	Communication and media studies	Economics
Dictionary of concepts in cultural anthropology. Winthrop, R.H. New York: Greenwood Press, 1991. *Atlas of world cultures.* Murdock, G.P. Pittsburgh: University of Pittsburgh, 1981. *A dictionary of world mythology.* Cotterell, A. New York: Putnam, 1980.	*Dictionary of communication and media studies.* 2nd edn. Watson, J. and Hill, A. London: Edward Arnold, 1989. *The communication handbook: a dictionary.* DeVito, J.A. New York: Harper & Row, 1986.	*Dictionary of economics.* Rutherford, D. London: Routledge, 1991. *The Collins dictionary of economics.* Pass, C.L., Lowes, B. and Davies, L. Glasgow: HarperCollins, 1993. *Everyman's dictionary of economics: an alphabetical exposition of economic concepts and their application.* London: J.M. Dent, 1976.
History	**Philosophy**	**Politics**
A dictionary of concepts in history. Ritter, H. Westport, Connecticut: Greenwood Press. Reference Sources in the Social Sciences, 1986. *A dictionary of Eastern European history since 1945.* Held, J. London: Mansell, 1994. *A dictionary of historical terms.* 2nd edn. Cook, C. London: Macmillan, 1989.	*A dictionary of philosophy.* 2nd edn. Lacey, A.R. London: Routledge & Kegan Paul, 1986. *Dictionary of theories (philosophy).* Bothamley, J. London: Gale, 1993. *The Oxford dictionary of philosophy.* Blackburn, S. Oxford: Oxford University Press, 1994.	*A dictionary of political analysis.* Roberts, G. and Edwards, A. (eds). London: Edward Arnold, 1991. *Political science thesaurus II.* 2nd edn. Beck, C. Pittsburgh: University of Pittsburgh, 1979. *A dictionary of modern politics.* 2nd edn. Robertson, D. (ed.). London: Europa Publications, 1993. *A dictionary of world politics: a reference guide to concepts, ideas and institutions.* Evans, G. and Newnham, J. Hemel Hempstead: Harvester Wheatsheaf, 1991.
Psychology	**Sociology**	**Religion and belief**
Dictionary of key words in psychology. Bruno, F.J. London: Routledge, 1986. *The dictionary of personality and psychology.* Rom, H. and Lamb, R. Oxford: Blackwell, 1986. *Dictionary of behavioral science.* Wolmer, B.B. (ed.). San Diego: Academic Press, 1989. *Penguin dictionary of psychology.* 2nd edn. Reber, A.S. London: Penguin, 1995. *A student's dictionary of psychology.* 2nd edn. Stratton, P. and Hayes, N. London: Edward Arnold, 1993.	*Penguin dictionary of sociology.* 3rd edn. Abercrombie, N. et al. London: Penguin, 1994. *Collins dictionary of sociology.* Jary, D. and Jary, J. London: HarperCollins, 1991. *Dictionary of quotations in sociology.* Bardis, P.D. Westport, Connecticut: Greenwood Press, 1985.	*Chambers dictionary of beliefs and religions.* Goring, R. (ed.). London: Chambers, 1992. *Macmillan dictionary of religion.* Pye, M. London: Macmillan, 1993.

Appendix 6: examples of subject encyclopaedias

Sociology	Anthropology	Language and linguistics
Encyclopedia of sociology. 4 vols. New York: Macmillan, 1992.	*The illustrated encyclopaedia of mankind.* 3rd edn. 22 vols. Carlisle, R. (ed.). London: Marshall Cavendish, 1990.	*The Cambridge encyclopaedia of language.* Crystal, D. Cambridge: Cambridge University Press, 1987.
The Macmillan student encyclopaedia of sociology. Mann, M. London: Macmillan Press, 1983.	*Encyclopedia of world cultures.* O'Leary, T.J. and Levinson, D. (eds). Riverside, NJ: G.K. Hall, 1991.	*An encyclopaedia of language.* Collinge, N.E. (ed.). London: Routledge, 1990.
Encyclopedia of feminist theories. Code, L. (ed.). London: Routledge, 1999.	*Encyclopedia of anthropology.* Hunter, D.E. and Whitten, P. (eds). New York: Harper, 1976.	*Encyclopedic dictionary of the sciences of language.* Ducrot, O. and Tzvetan, T. Baltimore, Maryland: Johns Hopkins University Press, 1981.
International encyclopaedia of propaganda. Cole, R. (ed.). London: Fitzroy Dearborn, 1998.	*Encyclopaedia of social and cultural anthropology.* Barnard, A. and Spencer, J. (eds). London: Routledge, 1998.	*The linguistics encyclopaedia.* Malmkjaer, K. London: Routledge, 1995.

Politics	Religion and beliefs	Psychology
The Blackwell encyclopaedia of political thought. Miller, D. (ed.). Oxford: Blackwell, 1987.	*Living religions: an encyclopaedia of the world's faiths.* Fisher, M.P. and Luyster, R.W. London: I.B. Tauris, 1990.	*Encyclopedia of psychology.* 4 vols. Corsini, R.J. (ed.). New York: John Wiley and Sons, 1984.
Encyclopaedia of political economy. 2 vols. O'Hara, P.A. (ed.). London: Routledge, 1999.	*The encyclopedia of religion.* 16 vols. Eliade, M. (ed.). New York: Collier Macmillan, 1987.	*The encyclopaedic dictionary of psychology.* Harry, R. and Lamb, R. (eds). Oxford: Blackwell, 1983.
Political and economic encyclopaedia of Western Europe. Nicholson, F. Harlow: Longman, 1990.	*The world Christian encyclopaedia.* 3 vols. Barrett, D. (ed.). Oxford: Oxford University Press, 1995.	*Encyclopaedia of psychology.* 2nd edn. 3 vols. Eysenck, H.J., Arnold, W. and Meili, R. London: Search Press, 1979.
Encyclopaedia of government and politics. 2 vols. Hawkesworth, M. and Kogan, M. (eds). London: Routledge, 1992.	*Companion encyclopaedia of theology.* Houlden, L. and Byrne, P. (eds). London: Routledge, 1995.	*Companion encyclopaedia of psychology.* 2 vols. Coleman, A.M. (ed.). London: Routledge, 1994.

Philosophy	Economics	Education
The Oxford companion to the mind. Oxford: Oxford University Press, 1987. *The encyclopaedia of philosophy.* Parkinson, G.H.R. (ed.). London: Routledge, 1990. *The concise encyclopaedia of Western philosophy and philosophers.* Urmson, J.O. (ed.). London: Hutchinson, 1960. *The Routledge encyclopaedia of philosophy.* 10 vols. Print and 1 CD ROM. Craig, E. (ed.). London: Routledge, 1998.	*Encyclopedia of economics.* Marshall, E.B. and Friedman, J.P. Boston: Waven, Gorham and Lamont, 1982. *Encyclopedia of economics.* Douglas, G. (ed.). New York: McGraw-Hill, 1982.	*The international encyclopaedia of education: research and studies.* 10 vols. Huson, T. and Postlethwaite, T.N. (eds). Oxford: Pergamon Press, 1985. *The international encyclopaedia of teaching and teacher education.* Dunkin, M.J. (ed.). Oxford: Pergamon Press, 1987.

Appendix 7: a selection of subject indexes and abstracts

Subject	Primary indexes & abstracts	Other indexes & abstracts
Anthropology	*Abstracts in anthropology* *American anthropological association abstracts*	*Sociofile*
Art and design	*Art & archaeology technical abstracts* *Avery index to architectural periodicals*	*British Humanities Index*
Economics	*Economic abstracts* *EconLit* *IntiEc* *ABI/Inform*	*Abstracts of working papers in economics* *Journal of economic literature* *Official index to the Financial Times* *The Financial Times on CD-ROM*
Education	*Current index to journals in education (ERIC)* *Sociology of education abstracts* *Multicultural education abstracts* *British education index*	*Education administration abstracts* *Special education needs abstracts* *Education technology abstracts* *Research into higher education abstracts* *School organization & management abstracts*
English	*Abstracts of English studies (ceased publ. 1991)* *English poetry database* *British Humanities Index* *Literary journals index full-text* *Year's work in English studies*	*Modern language review* *Language teaching* *ABELL – Annual bibliography of English language and literature* *Wilson essay and general literature index* *The Times literary supplement* *Literature online*
Health care	*Nursing research abstracts* *MIDIRS (Midwifery digest)* *Occupational therapy index* *Physiotherapy index* *Popular medical index*	*Sociological abstracts (Sociofile)* *Psychological abstracts*
History	*Historical abstracts*	*Dissertation abstracts* *Palmer's index to The Times*
Information science	*LISA* *ASLIB: current awareness abstracts* *Information science abstracts (ISA)* *Anbar (Information management & technology abstracts)*	*Current research in library & information science* *Children's literature abstracts* *Library literature* *Emerald full-text CD ROM*
Language and linguistics	*Linguistic abstracts* *Linguistic & language abstracts*	*Language teaching & linguistics abstracts* *Linguistics & language behavior abstracts*

Subject	Primary indexes & abstracts	Other indexes & abstracts
Leisure, tourism and sport	*Articles in hospitality & tourism* *Rural recreation & tourism abstracts* *Leisure recreation & tourism abstracts*	*Museum abstracts* *British Humanities Index*
Management and organizations	*ABI/Inform* *Complete ANBAR* *Institute of management international databases plus* *Emerald full-text CD ROM* *Business periodicals index* *The Financial Times on CD-ROM*	*Management & marketing abstracts* *Business publications index & abstracts* *Women in management review & abstracts* *Sociological abstracts (Sociofile)* *SCIMP (European index of management periodicals)* *Wilson business abstracts*
Media and communications	*Communication abstracts* *Sociological abstracts (Sociofile)* *Wilson social science abstracts*	*British Humanities Index*
Philosophy	*Philosopher's index*	*British Humanities Index*
Politics & government	*International political science abstracts* *PAIS international (Public affairs information service)* *ABC political science & government: a bibliography of contents*	*Sage public administration abstracts* *Urban abstracts* *LOGA (Local government annotations service)*
Psychology	*PsycINFO: Psychological abstracts*	
Religion & belief	*Religious & theological abstracts* *British Humanities Index*	*Guide to indexed periodicals in religion. Regazzi, J.J. & Hines, T.C. Metuchen, NJ: Scarecrow Press, 1975*
Social policy & welfare	*Sociological abstracts (Sociofile)* *Social service abstracts* *Health service abstracts*	*Social work research & abstracts* *Sage public administration abstracts*
Sociology	*Sociological abstracts (Sociofile)* *Wilson social science abstracts*	*Sage race relations abstracts* *Studies in women abstracts*
Women	*Studies on women abstracts* *Women's studies abstracts*	*Women in management review & abstracts* *Sociological abstracts (Sociofile)*

Appendix 8: Internet file types and applications

Type of resource	File extension	Full name	Application to use
Web pages	html, htm	Hypertext Markup Language	WWW browser
Text	txt	TeXT	Notepad
Documents	rtf	Rich Text Format	MS Word
	pdf	Portable Document File	Acrobat Reader
	ai, eps, ps	Postcript File	Postcript printer
	uue	UU encoded file	Wincode or UUdecode
Images	gif	Graphic Information Format	WWW Browser
	jpg, jpeg	Joint Picture Group	Graphic converter or Lview
	tiff, tif	Tagged Image Format	Desktop Publishing Package
	bmp	Bit MaPped	MS Paintbrush or Lview
Film clips	mov, qt	Moving Image	Quicktime
	mpg, mpeg	Motion Picture Group	Media Player or Sparkle
Sound	aiff	Apple File	Sound Machine
	au	Audio	Sound Media Player
	ra, ram	Real Audio	Real Player
	wav	WAV File	Sound Recorder
	tsp	TrueSpeech	True Speech Player
Files	zip	ZIPped	WinZip, Zipit or pkunzip
	Z	compressed file	decompress or uncompress

Internet address codes

Organization	UK	USA	Rest of world
Academic	ac	edu	au = Australia
Company	co	com	ch = Switzerland
Non-profit	org	org	de = Germany
Government	gov	gov	fr = France
Network	net	net	nl = Netherlands
Military		mil	ru = Russia

Appendix 9: Internet search profile

1 Topic descriptors
Write down all the words and phrases which can be used to describe your topic.
Identify terms that have too many meanings to avoid obtaining too many irrelevant results.
Use general topic descriptors if you want to do a general search.

2 Unique identifiers for the topic
Write down any unique words, phrases, acronyms and synonyms by which your topic and its related elements can be identified.
Make lists of your terms – those which will narrow your search and those which will broaden your search.
Use these to focus your search using addition and multiplication of terms.

3 People, organizations and associations
List any key people, organizations, such as research centres, and associations which are connected with your topic. If you do not know of any, come back to this box once you have found some during your search.
If you have the name of any organizations, put them in quotation marks.

4 Statement strings
Write down the statements you will use for your search using math symbols and Boolean operators.
Use your lists of terms to construct statements for searching.

5 Directories to be searched
Make a list of the directories which you will search.
If you have few results, use your list of terms to broaden your search.

6 Search engines to be searched
Make a list of the search engines which you will search.
If you have few results, use your list of terms to broaden your search.

Glossary

This is a list of some of the words and phrases used in this book. For further amplification and definitions of other words consult reference sources such as the following and others that you will find listed in Chapter 4, 'Quick reference materials'.

- **Caltech general reference page**.
  (address – http://library.caltech.edu/reference/default.htm).
  Useful set of links to a range of reference sources including encyclopaedias and dictionaries such as a hypertext *Webster's dictionary*. 🕸
- **Hypertext Webster interface dictionary and thesaurus**.
  (address – http://c.gp.cs.cmu.edu:5103/prog/webster/). 🕸
- **A web of online dictionaries**.
  (address – www.facstaff.bucknell.edu/rbeard/diction.html).
  Beard, R. 1996. This will search over 800 dictionaries, including etymological dictionaries, thesauri and the like in 150 languages, with preference given to free online sources. 🕸

Accession number	A number assigned to an item in a library and then recorded in an accession record.
Anthology	A book made up of a collection of extracts from various other works by a single author or other authors, selected by an editor or editors.
Appendix	A part of a written work that is added on to the main work, usually at the end; it is therefore not an essential part of the work but contains complementary information that is too long for footnotes.
Archives	A collection of non-current records produced by a person, body, organization, association, company and the like, deposited for preservation and collection for their historical value.
Article	A paper on a specific topic, such as an essay, normally published in a journal. It is refereed for quality by peers.
Bibliography	A list of sources cited (references) or referred to by an author of a work, usually at the end or

as footnotes. Also a list of sources on a topic by many authors, collected to form the knowledge on that topic.

Bibliometrics The use of statistical methods to analyse how materials are utilized in published work and research to show the influence of particular work and ideas.

Boolean logic A sub-set of logic developed in the nineteenth century by George Boole. It is now used to combine symbols for searching databases in a systematic way using logical operators (commands) normally made up of AND, NOT, NEAR and OR.

Browser A software program that enables the search of WWW documents, by decoding html-encoded files into text, images and sounds.

CD ROM Compact Disc Read Only Memory: a small plastic optical disc used to store digitized information.

Citation The bibliographical details of works used or referred to in the text, to show the source of ideas.

Conference paper A paper given at a meeting, often called by a professional or academic association, to exchange information, interpretations and research findings. Sometimes published as part of proceedings of the conference.

Copyright The right granted to the author(s) of a work restricting its use without permission and governed by copyright laws.

Critical annotation A short evaluative comment on references cited; or the bibliography of a work.

Criticism From the Greek *kritikos* meaning to judge. In writing, the clear and unbiased evaluation of a work from the standpoint of the aims of the author and using the canons of scholarship.

Cumulative index A series of indexes that have been published over time and have been combined into one index.

Digest An abridgement or condensation, longer than a synopsis, of a piece of work usually prepared by someone other than the author of the work.

Digitization The process of creating work in digital format or converting existing work from other formats into digitized format.

Directory A reference source of names, addresses and

	the like, or the name for the place where files are grouped together on a computer.
Dissertation	A lengthy piece of written work, circa. 15,000 words, usually based on research for a Master's degree from a university.
Domain name	The highest-level name of a web site that identifies a site.
Download	To transfer information from one computer to your computer or onto a floppy disk.
Editorial	A brief column normally written by the editor of a journal or newspaper that expresses an opinion on a current issue.
E-journal	A journal published electronically and made available via the Internet and that may have standards equivalent to print-based journals.
Fair use	Related to copyright laws which allow the fair use of a work produced by another. This is normally limited to quotation of 10 percent of the work.
Footnote	A reference placed at the bottom of a page to give a citation or to provide additional information about an author or work being used in the main text.
Gazette	A regularly published news sheet which records current events.
Ghost entry	A work referred to in a work, but one that has not been read.
Ghost writer	A person who writes a work on behalf of another.
Handbook	A reference source, usually compact, that provides factual information or guidance on a topic or subject.
Home page	The opening page of a web site that usually gives an overview of the whole site.
Index	An organized list of names, subjects or places that gives abbreviated references to the content of a work (e.g. book) or works in subject field (e.g. sociology).
Internet service provider	ISP: a company that provides access to the Internet.
ISBN	International Standard Book Number: a unique four-part, ten-digit code assigned to most books.
ISSN	International Standard Serial Number: a unique number assigned to serial publications (i.e. journals).

Journal	A regular publication, usually on a dedicated subject, that disseminates current research and thinking on a range of topics within a specific discipline.
Librarian	A person who works in a library and has detailed technical knowledge of how information is organized and can be accessed. An invaluable resource for the researcher.
Literature review	A critical evaluation and appraisal of work, including research, theory and argument, in a given subject field on a particular topic, usually undertaken for a graduate or post-graduate dissertation or thesis to show understanding of the field, the ability to criticize appropriately, and often to show the need for further research.
Literature search	A systematic and planned search for literature on a topic under investigation using all available bibliographic tools and informed sources, including experts in the field. Often used to produce a literature review.
Mediated search	A search for literature on a topic undertaken by another, such as a librarian, on one's behalf.
Monograph	A book on a specific topic that reports on research or makes an argument.
Newspaper	A daily or weekly publication on newsprint that reports on current events and carries advertising, cartoons, editorials, sports news and competitions. Newspapers are divided into tabloid (generally non-serious with little analysis) and broadsheets (with more depth and analysis).
OPAC	Online Public Access Catalogue: a library catalogue in electronic format.
Peer review	The process of ensuring the quality of an article by having it anonymously reviewed by peers of the author.
Periodical	A regular publication such as newspapers, newsletters, magazines and professional journals, which contain news, short articles, calendars of events and the like, and which are not normally peer-reviewed.
Plagiarism	Copying someone else's work and passing it off as your own.
Polemic	A debate or argument on a topic which challenges an accepted idea, theory or position.

Preface	A statement by an author or editor of a work at the beginning of the work that outlines its origins, purpose, scope and intended audience and is usually followed by acknowledgements.
Proceedings	The published record of a meeting, usually papers given at a conference or symposium.
Quotation	The words of another reproduced verbatim in one's own work. These are placed in quotation marks, or indented (if more than three lines) and are always cited in the references.
Synopsis	A short, non-evaluative statement containing the main points of a piece of work.
Syntax	The sequence or order in which terms are arranged, usually for searching a database.
Textbook	A book usually written for students that provides information and guidance on a subject or topic.
Thesis	A lengthy piece of work, usually for a doctoral degree from a university, that makes an original contribution to knowledge.
Underground press	Publications by not-for-profit organizations, normally outside of conventional bibliographical control (i.e. ISBNs), written with the purpose of forwarding a political or moral issue.
Virtual library	A collection of works and links to works that exist on the Internet but not in physical reality.

Index